GUARDIAN ANGELS BY MY SIDE

TRUE STORIES OF ANGELIC ENCOUNTERS AND DIVINE INTERVENTIONS

Barbara Love

WESTBOW
PRESS
A DIVISION OF THOMAS NELSON

Photo Credit: Redwood Studios, Grand Ledge, Michigan

WestBow Press books may be ordered through booksellers or by contacting:

WestBow Press
A Division of Thomas Nelson
1663 Liberty Drive
Bloomington, IN 47403
www.westbowpress.com
1-(866) 928-1240

ISBN: 978-1-4497-0753-8 (sc)
ISBN: 978-1-4497-0754-5 (e)

Library of Congress Control Number: 2010940009

Printed in the United States of America

WestBow Press rev. date: 11/04/2010

Contents

Introduction

$\mathcal{I}$ believe that God can heal and provide messages and instruction through his messengers, whom we call angels, because it happened to me. I believe that it was a test of my faith to see if I would listen, follow the directions and fully put my trust in God. He sent messages through his angels with instructions for my healing, and because I listened, I was healed. The angels told me that my story would be called "My Grace from God," which is the title of the first story included in this collection.

A few years later, my son Jacob, age six at the time, began suffering from awful night terrors. I will never forget the horrific screams I heard from my young son in the middle of the night. They continued on, night after night, for weeks. They were so upsetting to him that they not only left *him* with little sleep, but also the entire family. As he awoke screaming, nearly every night, I ran to his rescue. However, despite our efforts, the night terrors would not go away. Then, one night something miraculous happened. His angel appeared in his bedroom doorway, and this wonderful and blessed experience changed our lives.

When I began to tell others about my experience and about the appearance of Jacob's angel, I found that so many others also had amazing stories to share about life-changing divine interventions and angelic encounters. I felt that God was leading each one of these individuals to me for a particular reason. I began to pray about it, and I soon felt without a doubt that He wanted to use me to get their stories out to you.

As they shared their miraculous stories with me, many also shared that they had prayed that God would lead them to the right person so that their beautiful stories could be shared with others. Some of these compelling stories were lifesaving, and everyone one of them was life-changing. In most of these stories, an angel appeared in times of need, and in some stories, although an angel didn't appear in form, a divine intervention seemed to have taken place. Each one of these blessed events changed lives. Each divine story is spiritually uplifting and inspiring. I know as you read about each one of these beautiful and amazing divine interventions, you too will be inspired.

WHAT THE BIBLE TEACHES
US ABOUT ANGELS

*T*he word "angel" actually comes from the Greek word *angelos*, which means "messenger." The matching Hebrew word *mal'ak* has the same meaning. Angels appear in the Bible from the beginning to the end, from the book of Genesis to the book of Revelation. The Bible is our best source of knowledge about angels. For example, the book of Psalm indicates that humans have guardian angels. "For He shall give His angels charge over thee, to keep thee in all thy ways."(91:11)

Angels exist to praise God, and in doing so, they carry out God's direction and His commands. Angels are holy. God created them, and they cannot appear to us without God asking them to intercede in our lives. He has blessed us by providing each and every one of us guardian angels to guide and protect us throughout our lives, until the day when an angel leads us back to heaven to be reunited with God.

There are a great number of angels who live in God's great presence. They have tremendous power, and they possess superhuman intelligence. They can celebrate, have joy, hold conversations, and appear to people of all religions, even those of no religion at all, when God wants His people to listen.

Sometimes, humans who walk among us can appear as angels in disguise. As stated in Hebrews, "Let brotherly love continue. Be not forgetful to entertain strangers; for thereby some have entertained angels unawares" (13:1–2).

A Few Scriptural Passages on Angels

The Fall of Adam and Eve

Therefore the Lord God sent him forth from the garden of Eden, to till the ground from whence he was taken. So he drove out the man; and he placed at the east of the garden of Eden Cherubims, and a flaming sword which turned every way, to keep the way of the tree of life. (Genesis 3:23–24)

Jacob's Ladder

And Jacob went out from Beersheba and went toward Haran. And he lighted upon a certain place, and tarried there all night, because the sun was set; and he took of the stones of that place, and put them for his pillows, and lay down in that place to sleep. And he dreamed, and behold a ladder set up on the earth, and the top of it reached to heaven: and behold the angels of God ascending and descending on it! (Genesis 28:10–12)

God Sends an Angel to Lead Moses

Behold, I send an Angel before thee, to keep thee in the way, and to bring thee into the place which I have prepared. (Exodus 23:20)

The Book of Psalms

> The angel of the Lord encampeth round about them that fear him, and delivereth them. (Psalm 34:7)

> For he shall give his angels charge over thee, to keep thee in all thy ways. They shall bear thee up in their hands, lest thou dash thy foot against a stone. (Psalm 91:11–12)

The Angel Raphael

> I am Raphael, one of the seven angels who stand ever ready to enter the presence of the Glory of the Lord. (Tobit 12:15) NJB (New Jerusalem Bible)

The Angel Appears to Joseph

> Now the birth of Jesus Christ was on this wise: When as his mother Mary was espoused to Joseph, before they came together, she was found with child of the Holy Ghost. Then Joseph her husband, being a just man, and not willing to make her a public example, was minded to put her away privily. But while he thought on these things, behold, the angel of the Lord appeared unto him in a dream, saying, Joseph, thou son of David, fear not to take unto thee Mary thy wife: for that which is conceived in her is of the Holy Ghost. (Matthew 1:18–20)

Daniel in the Lion's Den

> Then the king arose very early in the morning, and went in haste unto the den of lions. And when he came to the den, he cried with a lamentable voice unto Daniel: and the king spake and said to Daniel, O Daniel, servant of the living God, is thy God, whom

thou servest continually, able to deliver thee from the lions? Then said Daniel unto the king, O king, live for ever. My God hath sent his angel, and hath shut the lions' mouths, that they have not hurt me: forasmuch as before him innocency was found in me; and also before thee, O king, have I done no hurt. (Daniel 6:19–22)

The Angel Gabriel Appears to Mary

And in the sixth month the angel Gabriel was sent from God unto a city of Galilee, named Nazareth, to a virgin espoused to a man whose name was Joseph, of the house of David; and the virgin's name was Mary. And the angel came in unto her, and said, Hail, thou that art highly favoured, the Lord is with thee: blessed art thou among women. (Luke 1:26–28)

An Angel Appears to the Shepherds

And there were in the same country shepherds abiding in the field, keeping watch over their flock by night. And, lo, the angel of the Lord came upon them, and the glory of the Lord shone round about them: and they were sore afraid. And the angel said unto them, Fear not: for, behold, I bring you good tidings of great joy, which shall be to all people. For unto you is born this day in the city of David a Saviour, which is Christ the Lord. And this shall be a sign unto you; Ye shall find the babe wrapped in swaddling clothes, lying in a manger. And suddenly there was with the angel a multitude of the heavenly host praising God, and saying, Glory to God in the highest, and on earth peace, good will toward men. (Luke 2:8–14)

The Resurrection of Jesus

But Mary stood without at the sepulchre weeping: and as she wept, she stooped down, and looked in the sepulchre, And seeth two angels in white sitting, the one at the head, and the other at the feet, where the body of Jesus had lain. And they say unto her, Woman, why weepest thou? She saith unto them, Because they have taken away my Lord, and I know not where they have laid him. And when she had thus said, she turned herself back, and saw Jesus standing, and knew not that it was Jesus. Jesus saith unto her, Woman, why weepest thou? Whom seekest thou? She, supposing him to be the gardener, saith unto him, Sir, if thou have borne him hence, tell me where thou hast laid him, and I will take him away. (John 20:11–15)

The Angel Rescues Peter from Jail

And, behold, the angel of the Lord came upon him, and a light shined in the prison: and he smote Peter on the side, and raised him up, saying, Arise up quickly. And his chains fell off from his hands. And the angel said unto him, Gird thyself, and bind on thy sandals. And so he did. And he saith unto him, Cast thy garment about thee, and follow me. And he went out, and followed him; and wist not that it was true which was done by the angel; but thought he saw a vision. When they were past the first and the second ward, they came unto the iron gate that leadeth unto the city; which opened to them of his own accord: and they went out, and passed on through one street; and forthwith the angel departed from him. (Acts 12:7–10)

Letter from Saint Paul to the Hebrews

> Let brotherly love continue. Be not forgetful to entertain strangers; for thereby some have entertained angels unawares. (Hebrews 13:1–2)

The Book of Revelation

> And when he had opened the seventh seal, there was silence in heaven about the space of half an hour. And I saw the seven angels which stood before God; and to them were given seven trumpets. (Revelation 8:1–2)

> And there was war in heaven: Michael and his angels fought against the dragon; and the dragon fought and his angels, and prevailed not; neither was their place found any more in heaven. (Revelation 12:7–8)

Chief among the angels, the archangel Michael is considered the greatest of angels. His name means, "Who is like God." He is an angel of repentance, mercy, and righteousness who appears in Islamic, Jewish, and Christian angelology, the study and doctrine of angels. Michael is often depicted with a sword, dressed in armor, and associated with shades of blue.

The archangel Gabriel presides over heaven, the prince of justice and chief of the angelic guards. His name means "God is my strength." He is a messenger angel who appeared to the Virgin Mary. Gabriel is the angel of annunciation, heavenly mercy, resurrection, and revelation. Gabriel will blow the horn announcing the second coming of Christ. In the Islamic tradition, Gabriel is the angel of humanity, the spirit of truth, and his symbol is the lily.

The archangel Raphael is the angel of healing. His name means, "God heals." He is the friendliest and merriest of all angels. Chief among the guardian angels, Raphael has the special charge of protecting the young, the innocent, and travelers. He is the angel of prayer, love, joy, light, providence, and healing. He is often shown carrying a pilgrim's staff. Many identify the color green with Raphael, perhaps to associate him with the healing of the earth.

Another archangel named Uriel, is often found in church dedications, art, and listed as one of the principal archangels. He is known as the angel of repentance. Uriel, is believed to be the angel who warned Noah of the flood. His name means, "God is light, or God is fire."

As you read these amazing stories of angel encounters, remember to give God the glory, for it is He who sent these angels on His behalf. Even the angels do not want the glory, as the book of Revelation states, "And I John saw these things, and heard them. And when I had heard and seen, I fell down to worship before the feet of the angel which showed me these things. Then saith he unto me, See thou do it not: for I am thy fellowservant, and of thy brethren the prophets, and of them which keep the sayings of this book: worship God." (Revelation 22: 8–9).

My Guardian Angel

My guardian angel,
sent from above,
a sign of God's eternal love.
My angel, I know you're always here.
With you beside me, I no longer have fear.
Help me to show others the love that you give
here on this earth, where I now live.
Watching and protecting,
guiding me along my way,
you are such a blessing,
I thank God and say,
"Thank you,
for my guardian angel by my side,
for she will forever be
my loving guide."

By: Barbara Love

My Grace from God

God wasn't ready for her just yet, and she wasn't yet ready to move on, either.

Besides, God had a special plan for her life. Her work was not yet done.

Headaches would come and go; they became part of my life, you could say. One day, I had a severe pain in the back of my head, about two inches in diameter. The pain was so intense, it felt as though my head would burst. I was very scared, as I was alone at the time with my two boys, ages one and four.

Too sick to walk, I crawled on the floor to my youngest son to change his diaper. Tears streamed down my face as I tried to bear the pain. I tried calling my husband, my relatives, and my neighbors, but no one could be reached. It was a Saturday morning and my doctor's office was closed. I knew I was in no shape to drive myself to the emergency room, which would also put my own sons' lives at risk. I called "Nurseline," a service that gave medical advice. I explained the awful pain as tears streamed down my face. I explained how I was dizzy and couldn't stand or walk and how I felt as though my head was going to burst. I told her of the stiffness in my neck and in my right arm. I answered all of the nurse's questions. She ended up replying, "We advise you get to the emergency room immediately."

I couldn't call an ambulance, as I had no one to watch my little ones, yet I knew I needed help immediately. I got out of the chair, crawled to my two boys, and grabbed one in each arm. I sobbed and prayed silently, *Please help me find someone, anyone, to get me to the hospital.* I then rang my sister again, and this time she answered. I told her I needed to get to the hospital and she replied, "I'll be there as soon as I can." She and her husband arrived a short time later. Meanwhile, a sense of God's peace came over me, calming me, and I felt everything was going to be okay.

Many tests followed that day, all of which came back negative. I was given a painkiller, and soon the pain subsided. Sometime after that, the pain and stiffness in my neck and right arm subsided, as well. I was discharged with no answers. I was frustrated yet relieved the pain had stopped so that I could go back home to my husband and children.

Though I did not realize it at the time, the pain wasn't gone forever. Because of the pain's severity, my body was very weak and tired, and I had to hire a sitter to watch my kids. I remained in bed for the following several days, trying to regain enough strength to go on about my daily activities.

Then another headache came, but this one was different. I soon learned it was a "spinal tap headache" from the spinal tap test I was given in the emergency room. I learned it would subside on its own, but it would take some time.

Monday arrived, so my husband took me in to see our family doctor. I tried sitting in the waiting room chair without falling out, but because I was so dizzy and weak, this was difficult. The room swirled and swirled. I kept thinking, *please call me back next … please*! Across the room, an elderly lady who was also waiting to see the doctor said quietly, "My gosh, I look at that woman and how sick she is and it makes me feel guilty for being here." Finally, the doctor called me back.

The doctor watched as I tried to walk down the hallway with help from my husband, and my doctor quickly said, "Lie down right now!" He took my blood pressure and began to panic. He said, "Your blood pressure is at a dangerous level; what is going on?" I didn't have a history of high blood pressure in my past. The doctor began to ask my husband questions about what medicine I was on. The only thing I was taking was birth control pills. He said, does she have them with her? My husband handed them to the doctor, and he threw them in the garbage. He then said, it is imperative that she rest in bed with no stress or distractions. He looked at my little ones and said, "Let Mommy rest. It's very important, okay?" He said it with such sternness that it left me worried if it was okay to go home in my condition, but despite my concern, I was sent home to rest. However, soon after, more problems arose.

Although the pain didn't come back, I then started having numbing and weakness on my right side. It started with my right pinky and then would spread through my hand, my right arm, then down my right leg, all the way to my foot, and then to the end of my toes. My doctor didn't have any answers at this point, and all the tests he suggested had already been done on me. He and all the emergency physicians were puzzled about what to do next.

The numbing would come and go often now, and I was scared for myself and for my family. Yet, still there were no answers. Where was I going to get these answers, and when would relief come?

A few days later, I received a phone call. My grandmother was having a heart attack! I called my friend, asked her to watch my boys, and off I went, praying all the way, *Please, dear God, let my grandma be all right. If it's her time, I'll have to accept it.* I left it all in God's hands as I continued the drive and turned on the radio. The song playing was, "Wild Angels." I felt that was a sign from God that she was going to be all right, and a sense of peace came over me. "Thank you, Jesus," I sighed in relief as I continued on toward the hospital.

As I walked into the hospital room, my grandma smiled and said, "Hi, Barbie, so glad you could come."

"Grandma, how are you doing?"

Being the funny lady she is, she said, "I think I know what's wrong with me, Barbie. I haven't eaten a thing since yesterday night!"

"Yes, I'm sure that *must* be what's wrong with you, Grandma," I said. Snickering, I told her, "Well, we can fix that," and I brought her a plate of food from the cafeteria. She ate like there was no tomorrow. After she ate, she smiled, and the pains slowly decreased enough for her to doze off into a deep sleep.

As I sat there next to my grandma, the numbing slowly started to creep back again on my right side. After a while, I began to get scared and contemplated whether I should tell the nurse or walk back to the emergency room. Given my luck in the past, I was feeling quite hopeless, so I decided I would just try to go back home and rest. I kissed my grandma and told her that I loved her and would be back later. Just then, my father arrived and offered to drive me home, but I said, "No, I'll be okay. I'll just go back home to rest, and I'll be fine." Although it was scary not knowing the cause of all this, I just didn't know where else to turn for help.

As I was driving home, I got within a few miles from picking up my boys when the numbing started to spread into my right cheek. I became scared and started praying, "Dear God, please let me get home safely." The right side of my tongue then went numb. That is when I started thinking, *Oh, dear God, this isn't good.* I was closer to my home than my friend's home and tried to decide which way would be better for me to take. I didn't want my boys to see me in this condition, but I couldn't stand the thought of going home alone for fear of what might happen. I decided to pray constantly out loud as I came closer and closer to my friend's home. I got within blocks of her home when my hearing went. I couldn't hear a thing. I braked and started to pull over to the side of the road. I screamed out loud, "No God, no, no!" I pulled back onto the road and kept driving despite my condition. It wasn't the smartest thing to do, but I felt I *had* to get to my boys. I drove the remaining few blocks and pulled into my friend's driveway. As I approached, my friend opened the door and I must have looked like a ghost, because she said, "Lie down right here and don't get up." She called my husband, took my blood pressure, and I soon ended up an hour and a half away at a very large university hospital.

By the time we arrived, I couldn't walk and was placed into a wheelchair. My neck was so stiff I couldn't turn to the right or the left. I was so frustrated and ill. Again, we went through all the questions and tests with no answers, and again, the doctors were puzzled. They set up an appointment for me to see their specialist two days later and sent me home, where all the symptoms eventually subsided again. When I went back to see the specialists, they went through all my records, cat scans, MRIs, and past history. They then did many more tests to rule out multiple sclerosis and other possibilities. Four to five hours later, I was sent away with another painkiller to "stop the vein pulsations in my head" that they believed could be causing the numbing and the spells.

I took the medicine faithfully, but soon the symptoms began again. I felt so out of hope. Frustrated and upset, as I felt I had the best specialists' opinions, I knew the medicine wasn't helping.

In the early morning on my wedding day, five years before my illness, my mom called me. "Barbie, I've got some bad news. Aunt Lilly has been in an awful car accident. They're not sure if she is going to make it. I don't know what to do," she said. She told me that my aunt had gone out with friends and had been in an accident on the way home. A helicopter had taken her to the best hospital in a bigger nearby town. "I don't know whether I should be by *her* side or attend *your* wedding," my mom said. I told her, "By all means, go and be by her side!" It hurt so much, knowing I couldn't be there with her and that I wouldn't be able to have my own mother attend my wedding.

As Aunt Lilly lay there in a coma, hooked to machines, with her entire head swollen, the family stood at her bedside praying. The doctors said to prepare for the worst. They said that her injuries were so severe; it wasn't likely she would ever wake up again.

My wedding went on as planned. Half of the family continued to stand around Lilly's bedside, and the other half attended my wedding. Then, at the church, as the wedding time approached, I looked up to find my mother walking toward me. I said, "What are you doing here? You should be with Lilly."

My mother said, "She awoke from the coma and the doctors said it looks like she *will* make it!"

"Oh, that is wonderful!" I replied.

When she awoke from the coma, the first words out of Aunt Lilly's mouth were, "What are all of you doing here? It's Barbie's wedding day!"

Bewildered, they replied, "Don't you understand? We didn't expect you to awaken!"

Aunt Lilly said, "That's crazy, now go on and get out of here and be with Barbie; this is her wedding day! I'll be just fine! *I'm* not going *anywhere!*"

God wasn't ready for her just yet, and she wasn't ready to move on, either. Besides, He had a special plan with her life. Her work was not yet done. Some relatives left to attend my wedding and others stayed with her, but we all continued to pray for Aunt Lilly's complete recovery.

Through the pain, suffering, and the long road to recovery that this terrible accident caused in my aunt's life, she became in touch with her spirituality. Things began happening, she began to see visions from heaven and angels. She didn't talk about it at first, as she didn't understand what was occurring. Angels and spirit guides started appearing to her with wisdom from God and she was given advice for others' healing and spiritual development.

My mother, who was close to Aunt Lilly, spent a lot of time with her and soon began to realize her sister's wonderful God-given gift to help others. After my frustrating experience with the specialists' and their ineffective medical treatment of my mystery illness, my mom advised me, through the help of my aunt, to seek some advice from the angels and spirit guides, from the light and love of God. I believed if we opened our hearts and trusted in God, He could do great things. This is when my own miraculous healing began.

One day, my mother informed me she was going to Aunt Lilly's to visit. I said, "Could you please ask her to ask the angel guides for some advice regarding my condition? Please ask them if I'm on the right medication for my problem." I had just experienced dizzy spells walking out to my garden and back up to my house, and I was feeling very nauseas and light-headed.

My mother and my aunt were not aware of the specific medications I was on at that time, but I trusted that the angels knew. I was right, as evidenced in the angel's reply to my mother: "She is on two medications. One is a painkiller and the other one is supposed to be helping her condition. The painkiller isn't hurting her, but the other medicine, is hurting her and making her condition worse. It's causing more blood to enter the vein in her head, which could burst. Tell her to stop the medicine immediately and that she could die if she doesn't. Tell her to start taking an herb right away called 'ginkgo biloba.' Tell her to take two pills a day for thirty days and then one pill a day for six more months, and she will be healed."

I went out to the nearest health food store, purchased the herb, and headed back home. I started thinking that taking this herb would mean I would indeed have to stop the medications the doctor had prescribed for me. That was a bit scary, yet I wasn't getting better anyhow. Even then, I was still a bit apprehensive and wasn't sure if I was making the right decision. I was still feeling terrible, and I felt very strongly that He was leading me to stop my medication. The doctors told me my condition was not life-threatening. God's angel told me that with the current medication I was on, it was life-threatening. This was strictly my own decision to put my life in God's hands. I decided to stop the medications and try the herb.

The first day, I had no headache, no numbing, no weakness or dizziness, and I felt okay. I continued with the herb and without medication. My aunt then consulted the angels again who replied, "In five days, she will notice her energy increasing."

Oh my gosh, did I ever! I started to feel alive and energized beyond belief. I soon found myself cleaning my house, organizing, and straightening my closets and dresser drawers! I even had enough energy to work in the yard and do some planting—and all of this on the *same* day! I was so full of energy that I was bursting with happiness and renewed hope. I listened and put my trust in God, and through the help of His messengers, the angels, I was healed. I felt wonderful, and to this day, the symptoms have never again returned.

Sometimes, the answer to our problem can be a rather simple one. If we ask in faith, God will direct us to the source of information we are seeking. We need to quiet our hearts and minds, BELIEVE, pay attention, listen, and follow His leads for the answers we seek in our lives. We must practice to be still, for God speaks in whispers and it's a noisy world we live in. One of my favorite verses is in the book of Psalm, "Be still, and know that I am God." (46:10) When we *believe* that miracles *can* happen in our lives, they will begin to happen!

And I say unto you, Ask, and it shall be given you; seek, and ye shall find; knock, and it shall be opened unto you.

Luke 11:9

᪥ Barbara Love

Jacob's Angel

A mother's prayer is one of the strongest prayers in heaven.

*M*y son Jacob, age six, had been suffering from awful night terrors. For several weeks, he would awaken terrified in the middle of the night, screaming out in horrific screams. I remember him saying, "Don't turn out the light ever again, Mommy, because I will never again go back to sleep!"

He would awaken and cry repeatedly, and as a mom, I felt helpless. He was so terrified and disturbed that we knew what he was experiencing wasn't just his imagination. We just didn't know how to make whatever was terrifying him stop scaring him. He said that scary beings would shake him, waking him up and not letting him go back to sleep. I put a Bible under his pillow, and we would say our prayers morning and night, yet he continued to be awakened by these scary, evil beings.

Night after night, for weeks on end, it continued. Right about midnight, he would sit up screaming, scared out of his mind. I tried staying calm, praying with him, and reassuring him that nothing could ever hurt him and that everything was going to be okay, but he just pleaded in reply, "Just make them stop, Mommy. Please make them stop! I just want to sleep!"

I wanted so much to make them stop, but nothing I tried worked. I was completely out of answers and totally frustrated.

My mother said, "Pray for his angel to come and protect him."

I told her I *had* prayed, but that particular night we *both* prayed especially hard that his angel would come and protect him from whatever was causing these horrific night terrors. I had read somewhere before that a mother's prayer is one of the strongest prayers in heaven. I knew that soon, near midnight, Jacob would awaken me as usual, so I decided I would pray nonstop as midnight continued to approach.

I must have prayed myself to sleep, because I found myself awakened the next morning by Jacob's little voice. "Mommy, Mommy I saw my angel!" he said. His voice was excited and his face beamed as he told me his story with amazing detail. It was as if he was describing a much-desired shiny new bicycle under the tree on Christmas morning. This is how he explained what happened: "I was sleeping when I was awakened by these sparkly lights above my head and in front of me. I sat up, and the lights went 'swoosh' to the doorway of my room, and there she was, an angel! A real angel! She was really tall and had on a white dress with really big wings. The angel's head went all the way to the ceiling and her wings were the same colors as the sparkles I saw! They were see-through and like ... like the colors in the rainbow!"

Jacob went on and on describing what he had seen. "The angel had your color of hair, Mommy, same as *you*," he said, "and was really pretty in a bright light. The sleeves went down to here," he said as he took his little hand to his elbow. "Her hair went to here," again motioning with his hands near his shoulder. "She had a white belt on, like a rope, the same color as her dress, going all the way around here," he said, motioning a belt around his waist. His face glowed with excitement, and I had no doubt that what he had seen was truly his angel. As I continued to listen, I thanked God for answering his mother's prayer. I knew then that everything was going to be okay. I could see it all over my son's face!

Weeks and years then passed by, and not one night terror returned. Jacob no longer awoke screaming in fear. One day, when I was looking at a picture of an angel, Jacob came up behind me and shouted, "That's it, Mommy! That's like the angel I saw, but the wings had gold around the outside, and they moved just like a butterfly's does."

Praise God, He answered our prayers by sending His angel. Jacob's been forever changed since then. For years after that encounter, he occasionally saw beautiful angels. What a wonderful gift! I believe God left him with that ability as a blessed reminder that He will always protect Jacob with His angels.

One day sometime later, Jacob's little brother said, "I'm scared!" I heard Jacob reply, "You don't need to be scared. Don't you know we all have angels that are here to protect us?"

And all things, whatsoever ye shall ask in prayer, believing, ye shall receive.

Matthew 21:22

❧ Barbara Love

A Walk with the Angels

Their skin was more beautiful than any woman's, and the glow that emanated from them told me who they were.

It was a beautiful spring day in May. I had been feeling so wonderful because I had recently received Jesus Christ as my Lord and Savior. He washed away all my sins. The whole world seemed sweeter and lighter. My past was full of pain and nightmares, but now life was wonderful! I knew my life was going to get better and more wonderful with every passing day.

I had no idea that this particular day in May was one that I would remember for eternity! I had decided that since it was so beautiful outside, I would go for a walk. My two little girls, Brooke and Brianna, were in school. I put on a light jacket and headed out the door, grabbing my MP3 player on my way out so I could have some uplifting music to listen to as I walked and enjoyed the beautiful day.

As I walked, I noticed how gorgeous all the trees and flowers were. I am blessed that where I live, the neighborhood has nice foliage growing all around. I could see the Lord in everything that grew all around me as if for the first time. I stopped to examine some of the leaves on a plant and could see a cross or a star in every one of them. This excited me and filled me with such joy!

I continued on my walk and began to feel peace and joy from above. It was incredible! I was being enveloped by this wonderful warm sensation. I closed my eyes so that I could enjoy it more as I continued to walk, not even thinking that I was walking down the street blind in the natural sense. Some places along the walk had no sidewalks, so I was at the edge of the street. I had no concern about it at the time. I continued to bask in the glory I was feeling. It was so peaceful and refreshing.

As I was walking, I became aware that there were others suddenly at my side, one to my left and one to my right. While I was still walking with my eyes closed, the grace of God allowed me to see my visitors. Walking beside me was two of the most beautiful creatures I had ever seen! I would say that they were about eight feet tall. The one on my right had dark hair, while the one on my left had strawberry blonde hair. Their skin was more beautiful than any woman's, and the glow that emanated from them told me who they were. Their faces were the most beautiful I had ever seen. Their shoulders were very broad. They had wings that I heard swish as they came up beside me. Their wings were high above their heads and curved down gracefully to their feet.

They smiled a most beautiful and joyful smile as they each nodded at me. I was so elated, I felt that if I smiled any harder my face would crack in half. Talk about being full of joy! I put out both of my hands in order to hold each of their hands. I wanted all I could get out of the experience. I walked like this all the way down the street, feeling as if

I were floating on air, never once opening my eyes to see where I was. I didn't care! I knew I was in blessed hands. I would estimate that the entire walk with these angels of the Lord was about twenty minutes long. Near the end of the walk, I felt led to open my eyes for a quick second to see what I could see. What I saw was the top of the trees on my street! Then I quickly squeezed my eyes shut, but I could still see all that was going on around me.

Later, I remembered that while I had been with the angels, there had been a couple of cars that passed by. I could see the expressions on the drivers' faces as they saw me walking with my hands outstretched and eyes closed! I am sure they wondered what I was doing, as I assumed they could not see the beautiful angels beside me. When it was over, I was on the sidewalk in front of my house. This experience was so very intense and vivid, something that I will never ever forget! I feel so blessed to have walked with the angels that day!

ॐ Nancy,
California

*For He shall give his angels charge over
thee, to keep thee in all thy ways.*

Psalm 91:11

My Father's Love

One night, after about fifteen days of prayer, my dad was in his bedroom, praying and pleading for my life to be spared, when the room suddenly got really bright.

It was New Year's Eve, and the neighborhood was holding a big party. I was just a little girl, about six years old at the time. My oldest brother and some of his classmates were going off to serve in the Vietnam War, so the whole senior class was there to celebrate and wish them well with a going away party.

At the stroke of midnight, my daddy took me outside to shoot off sparklers. We stood near the front porch of the house. As we stood there, my dad saw a flame coming from the sky down toward us. He tried to stop it, but was unable to get there on time. It landed in between my coat collar and neck and blew up. This was no ordinary firecracker; it was a class A M-80. About eight of them are equal to a stick of dynamite, which is why they are now outlawed. All I remember was the smell of burning flesh and hair. Then, I went into cardiac arrest. My dad ran into the house with me and began CPR while my mother called the ambulance.

Upon my arrival at the hospital, the doctors told my parents that I was not going to make it through the night. They were able to get a heartbeat back, but the machines verified I was brain-dead. I made it through that night and somehow slipped into a coma. All EEGs still read that I was brain-dead, and other tests proved me to be deaf. My daddy cried and prayed each night that God would not take me. He was not a very religious man at that time.

One night, after about fifteen days of prayer, my dad was in his bedroom, praying and pleading for my life to be spared, when the room suddenly got really bright. A very calming feeling of warmth came over him. He then knew in his heart that I was going to be okay.

The very next day, when he came to the hospital, he walked into the ICU and found me sitting up and talking. I was begging for food and clothes. The doctors and nurses were awestruck, because I wasn't expected to ever wake up. There had been evidence that I was indeed brain-dead! By some miracle, there have been no lasting effects from this tragedy.

While I was in a coma, I took a trip to heaven. The angels told me it was not my time to go and that God needed me here on earth for a reason. I was told I had to go back and find my purpose. I was then delivered back to earth by one of God's angels. When I awoke that day, I awoke not only physically, but also spiritually! I felt renewed and blessed to have been given another chance to fulfill God's purpose for me here on earth.

Many people have come to me for inspiration. Every chance I get, I spread God's love and His word. I know this is part of what God wants of me. I am a child of God, and I live each and every day for Him.

Since this occurrence, my dad has passed away and is now home in heaven with Jesus. I know that my dad and the angels are watching over me, guiding me along my journey here on earth. The next time the angels welcome me into heaven, my dad will be right there beside them, and I will dwell with them and God for eternity.

ൠ Ellen,
Alabama

I waited patiently for the LORD; and he
inclined unto me, and heard my cry.

Psalm 40:1

Back Home

*I remember feeling a sense of peace come over me, and
then I saw them, the beautiful countless angels.*

It was a normal Monday morning routine here at home
in Florida, and I was getting prepared to drive my son
to school. We headed out on our northbound route, when I
came upon a four-way stop. I saw another car heading east,
whose driver failed to stop and ended up colliding with
us. Our car did a complete circle, and my head slammed
through the driver's side window.

I remember feeling a sense of peace come over me, and
then I saw them, the beautiful countless angels. I felt so
comfortable and peaceful in their presence; I knew I was in
heaven. I felt completely satisfied at the time and felt ready
to say goodbye to my family and my life on earth. I asked
if I could see my other relatives there in heaven, and my
request was granted. I wasn't at all afraid and never wanted
to leave that peaceful place. Another angel then approached
me and said, "You must fight to stay alive, to be with your
children. You must help find the missing children on earth.
This is God's plan for you. You must go back."

The next thing I recall was opening my eyes and seeing a very teary-eyed police officer asking me for my name. I felt so much pain, I couldn't think. About five minutes later, my name came to me. "Dawn," I said. "My name is Dawn." I was then taken away by ambulance to the nearest hospital, where I discovered my condition. I was suffering from a concussion and mild amnesia, but managed not to have a scratch on me! My son was also fine.

It would take several months for me to heal physically; but I felt awakened spiritually. This experience changed my life. I saw a bit of heaven and the angels and was told to go back and complete God's plan for my life. Since then, I've been determined to do just that—to find missing children and to reunite them with their families.

I thank Jesus for giving me the wonderful opportunity. I now know that when it is my time to go back home to heaven, I will be ready, knowing I've done so much to help the missing children here on earth.

ॐ Dawn,
Florida

And I beheld, and I heard the voice of many angels
round about the throne and the beasts and the elders;
and the number of them was ten thousand times
ten thousand, and thousands of thousands.

Revelation 5:11

DOMINGO'S DREAM

He could make out several robed figures
standing in front of the altar.

One of them, clothed in white, turned toward him,
and Domingo heard, in his soul rather than in his
ears, a summons: "Come unto me, little one."

*D*omingo crouched low in the weeds, the water of the Rio Grande lapping at his ankles. Had his mother been there, she would be scolding him for getting his shoes all wet. But, she was not. She was a many-days' walk to the south, worried sick for the son she knew had run away to the north.

Domingo knew it would be daylight soon, as the roosters from the nearby farm were just starting to crow. He knew he would have to cross the river before daybreak, or the Federals would surely catch him. He shivered, not from the cold, but from fear—fear of the Federals, the Border Patrol. The strange English words echoed in his mind. He had listened as men told their stories of swimming the big river and making a lot of money. They had spoken of the Border

Patrol Agents who must not catch you, or you would come back to Mexico without money, a failure.

I must not fail, Domingo thought, *I must get money.* Money for his grandma, whose legs didn't work and needed to see a doctor; money for his baby sister, whose cough never went away; and money for food. Food to stop the gnawing hungers, the hunger that never stopped unless he was asleep. Just as the first faint pink shade appeared in the sky, Domingo plunged into the river. It was not cold at all. Domingo loved the water. At home, he swam whenever he could in the creek near his uncle's home. He was a strong swimmer, and he was on the other side very quickly. It was called the big river, but it really wasn't.

He crawled out of the water, very wet and very proud. He was in the United States. He would get a job, get lots of money, and go back to his neighborhood with a big truck full of food. Nobody would ever be hungry again when Domingo got there with his truck.

Suddenly, a shaft of bright light cut across Domingo's path through the low brush and came to rest on his face, blinding him. "Freeze, wetback," said a voice behind the light, "just don't move. Look it here, Ned, we got a little one this time."

Another light swept Domingo's face as a second voice said, "Federal officers of the Immigration and Naturalization Service. You are hereby detained until your legal right to remain in this country can be determined."

Domingo didn't understand a word. But he knew he had been caught. He had failed. The lights dropped from his face, and strong hands clamped onto both of his arms and began to lead him through the brush. As it grew lighter,

Domingo could see that his captors, two big, uniformed *officers*," both carrying guns, were leading him toward a pale green passenger truck parked in the brush some distance away. On the door of the truck was a large blue circle with gold lettering. He couldn't read the words, but he didn't need to. Police cars always looked the same. He began to cry softly to himself. All his plans were turning into dust.

As they neared the patrol truck, one officer released him and began to walk around the front to the driver's door and opened it. He got inside the truck and reached through to release the lock on the passenger door. Suddenly a voice, rough and electric, came out of the truck. "Request immediate backup, we spotted four or five Hispanic males moving rafts across the river. They appear armed with automatic weapons. "Kennedy and Sorenson request immediate backup, on the double!"

Domingo could sense the tension in the new voice, even though he didn't understand the words. The hand on his arm was barely there as the second officer leaned toward the truck to better hear what the radio was saying. Domingo didn't have the slightest idea what was happening, but he knew he had a chance to escape. He wriggled out of the hand and started running for all he was worth. The agent felt him slip out of his grip and swore softly as he saw the youngster run away. But armed drug-runners were much more important to capture than wetbacks. He jumped into the truck as it roared into life. Dust spun from the wheels as they sped off toward their fellow officers. When you called for back up, you got back up.

Domingo ran and ran and ran. He ran faster and harder than he did the time his older brother chased him with the dead rattlesnake. He ran until he could not breathe. He collapsed against a mesquite tree and just lay there against it, gulping in air. Little by little, his breath came back to him. Domingo remembered how his mother was always reminding him that he had an angel watching over him, keeping him from harm. Domingo thanked the angel and pushed himself off the tree.

It was full daylight now, and Domingo could see cars moving on a small road several hundred yards away, through the scrub. He moved quickly and silently through the low trees, keeping an eye out for pale green trucks with big blue circles on the door. He said a little prayer to his angel to help him be watchful and walked out onto the shoulder of the road.

Now, thought Domingo, *it is time to find work.* He would do anything, anything at all, to make money. He was a good worker and a hard worker. What he wanted to find most of all was somebody who would give him a chance to show what he could do and pay him some money, to do it.

So, Domingo plodded on down the dusty little South Texas road, looking for work. Cars and trucks whizzed by him and paid him little, if any, notice. Once, he had to jump out of the way of a large green tractor pulling an even larger machine behind it. The driver of the tractor yelled at him, in Spanish, to watch where he was walking or he would be hurt. Domingo yelled back at him that his angel wouldn't let him get hurt, because he had to be strong to get money to take back to Mexico. The driver just shook his head and kept pulling the huge disc harrow down the road.

A little further along, Domingo saw an old man working with a hoe in a large, well-kept field. When he got near to the man, he called out in Spanish, "Tell me, Mr., do you have work for me?"

The old Mexican straightened slowly from his weed tending and, glad for the break in his monotonous routine, said, "Yes, my son, I have much work. I can give you work from sunrise to sunset. But I can give you no money. My *Boss* will not give money to a boy who cannot work as hard or as long as a grown man."

"I can work very hard, Sir," said Domingo, "because I must earn money to buy a truckload of food to take back to my family."

"My son," asked the man, "did you swim the Rio Grande to come and find work?"

"Yes, Sir."

"Many years ago, I swam the river to make much money in the land of the gringos. I work hard and long, and so does my wife, who does sewing. Together, we make only enough to live. We have no truck, only a little house and a little food."

"But are there no rich people who will pay you much money for work?"

"If you can find them, and if they will give you much money for work, perhaps. But I do not know where they are."

"My angel will help me find them," Domingo said. "My angel always helps me."

"*Good luck*," said the old man, as he went back tending to his weeds.

Once again, Domingo walked. He stopped several more times and asked his questions about work. He always got the same answer. Yes, there is work. No, there is no money.

Slowly, it began to dawn on him that he was in the wrong place. Farms and ranches did not have money. It must be in the cities, where the rich people were. Domingo knew he had to find such a city. Yet the longer he walked, the more his old friend hunger walked with him. Domingo knew many tricks to forget his old friend, and one by one he used them up. Of course, hunger had brought his good friend thirst with him. Thirst was much harder to forget than hunger.

By now, Domingo had come to the outskirts of a town. There were more and more buildings and less and less open land. Thirst was really pushing him hard now. Pushing him so hard that he jumped a small fence into a yard where a hose was running on some flowers. He grabbed the hose and drank and drank and drank. It was running quite slowly, taking a long time to rid him of hunger's good friend, when he heard a Spanish voice from behind him say, "Pretty thirsty, huh, wetback?" His lips curling around the word for wetback.

Domingo looked up slowly to see a big teenage boy with slicked back hair and sunglasses. "Stand up," he said.

Domingo did as he was told. The teenager moved directly in front of him and gazed down at him coolly. Not knowing anything else to say, Domingo asked him where he could find work. The older boy laughed and said, "Not in my grandmother's yard and probably not anywhere else." There are lots of people who live here who want work, and they don't like you coming over the river and trying to get the jobs they want. Best thing you can do is to go get your back wet again and go home. All you're gonna find here is trouble. Now beat it!"

Domingo moved to climb back over the fence. The older boy grabbed him by the shoulder, saying, "Not that way," He pointed to the front gate. "Use the gate and go home!"

Domingo ran to the gate, flung it open, and was once again walking down the road. He wasn't any closer to his dream, but at least he wasn't thirsty anymore. He *was* hungry, though—very hungry. Soon he came to a small store surrounded by shiny *American* cars and trucks. Domingo thought they were very beautiful—especially one bright blue pickup, whose driver was just getting back inside. Domingo went up to the driver and asked him where he could buy such a truck. The man looked at him and with a laugh said, "San Trejos Motors. Use your credit card to make the down payment," he yelled in Spanish, as he slammed the door in Domingo's face. The pickup roared into life and sprang backward, tires squealing, almost knocking Domingo to the ground. Domingo thanked his angel for protecting him once again. He went into the store. There was a young girl behind the counter. He went over to her and asked if he could buy something to eat.

"What would you like?" she asked, motioning with her hand toward the many racks of food in the store. Domingo looked around at the many different kinds of food. Most of the packages were a mystery to him, as their labels were written in English.

"I want *"patatas fritas,"* he said to her.

"Potato chips? Over there," she said, pointing to a rack full of large shiny bags.

Domingo went to the rack and took down a bag full of potato chips. Then he went back to the counter and laid it down. He pulled out ten large brass peso coins, his entire life's savings, worth about thirty-five cents in American money, and put it next to the bag.

"Sorry, little one," the girl said. "We don't take pesos."

Domingo didn't know what to do except to tell her that the coin was all the money he had and that he was very hungry. The girl reached under the counter and pulled out something wrapped in foil. "This is a taco from yesterday," she said. "I don't think anyone will miss it. Take it and go. I don't want my boss to find you here."

Domingo said, "Gracias," and went back outside. He unwrapped the taco and ate it very quickly. It was cold, the tortilla was hard, but at least it filled him up, and he could forget his old friend hunger for a while.

Domingo spent the rest of the day searching for work. He might as well have been searching for the lost city of El Dorado. The only thing he found were people who said, "No, no," and "Go away." The sun was starting to go down. He was very tired, and his companion, hunger, was demanding loudly that Domingo remember him again. He came to another market with several trashcans in front of it. One of them didn't have a lid, and Domingo dug into it. It was not the first time he had dug into a trashcan for food. He found some stale donuts. As he was pulling them out, the door to the market opened, and once again he heard the now very familiar, "Go away!"

He kept on. It was getting quite dark. He found himself by a small lake. There were several large bushes there with grass growing underneath them. He lay down on the grass and wondered to himself, *Where is the work? No one has any job for me. Had the men who crossed the river before me been telling the truth? How could they find work when I can find none?* He was confused and very sad. Had his angel forgotten him? Where was she now when he needed her most? Would he ever make some money? Without money, there would be no truck full of food for his family and neighbors. His dream would fail. He began to cry softly to himself. As the tears slid down his cheeks, Domingo slid into sleep. At least in sleep, he could have his dream.

In his dream, Domingo found himself in front of a great cathedral. It flowed with light, and it was very beautiful. He went through the ornately carved front door and stood at the beginning of a long walkway that led to a large candlelit altar. The interior of the cathedral was filled with a soft golden light. He could make out several robed figures standing in front of the altar. One of them, clothed in white, turned toward him, and Domingo heard, in his soul rather than in his ears, a summons: "Come unto me, little one."

He began to walk down the aisle with a tread so light that he almost felt as if he were floating. As he approached the altar, he saw that there were two ladies, both clothed in white, standing before him. One was facing him, and the other was turned toward the altar, her head bent in adoration. The one facing him had a look of great compassion, and her face was suffused with a golden glow. She spoke to him with a soft, sweet voice that echoed in his soul, "There is no need for sorrow, little one, for one as courageous and pure as you cannot but succeed in your quest. Thou shalt have thy dream."

Domingo knew without asking that this was his angel. He dropped to his knees and bent his head in prayer. He felt a hand being laid gently on his head and he felt, in the depths of his being, the light of his angel flowing through him. He raised his head to see that the other lady had also turned toward him. Her face also shone with light and love. Domingo knew her also, for hers was the face of the Blessed Virgin, which he had seen many times before.

Suddenly, Domingo was jerked from sleep by a loud crashing noise. He didn't know where he was—most of him was still in his dream. He shook his head and rubbed his eyes. What had happened? Where was his angel? He heard screams, which he didn't understand, but he could feel the urgency in the voice. He jumped to his feet and ran toward the screams. In the darkness, he could just barely make out a lady lying on the ground on the bank of the lake, screaming and shaking her hands toward the water. He looked out into the water and saw a car sinking slowly into it. Domingo knew that the lady was not screaming for herself, but for someone in the car. He could see head and shoulders sticking out of the water. Domingo reached through the open car window and released the baby from the small car seat, which had trapped it. He pulled the baby out and went to swim to shore, but he couldn't move. His pant leg had caught something on the car. He was being pulled under with the car. He put the baby on top of the car and yanked at his pants, trying to free himself.

Domingo was suddenly aware of bright lights coming from the bank. He felt the water over his head and then he only saw blackness. Once again, Domingo found himself in the golden cathedral with his angel and the Virgin Mary. He knew that he must have drowned. But how could he have his dream if he was in heaven? "Fear not, little one," he felt the angel say, "you are not dead, only dreaming, but your dream *is* your destiny. You will succeed, for you follow the way of the Savior: you place the welfare of others before your own."

Domingo awakened slowly, his head spinning. He was not in the cathedral in heaven, but in a bed in a room full of strange and wonderful things. A lady was bending over him, a lady dressed all in white. She looked like his angel, for her face had the same devoted compassion in it.

"Are we still in heaven, angel?" he asked her.

"No, we are in the hospital, and I'm not an angel. I'm a nurse. You almost drowned saving a baby's life. If the police hadn't gotten there when they did and revived you, you would surely be with the angels."

Domingo was pleased the nurse could speak Spanish. Then slowly, Domingo began to separate his dream from what had happened to him. He remembered the crash and the screaming lady and pulling the baby from the car. The door to the room opened, and another lady entered. She too was dressed in a white gown and there were white bandages on her head and arm. As she neared the bed, Domingo could see that she was not Mexican like most of the people he'd met since swimming the river. Instead, she was a white lady.

"Is this the one, nurse?" asked the Anglo lady. "Is this the boy that saved my baby's life?"

"Ma'am, you shouldn't be here," answered the nurse. "You have been injured and you should be in bed. Yes, this is the boy."

The white lady walked over to Domingo's bed and put her hand on his forehead. "I don't know who you are or how you came to be there by the lake. But it must surely be providence, and you have my eternal gratitude, young man."

Domingo did not understand her words, but he felt her warmth and her gratitude. He could only gaze at her blankly, for he did not know how to answer.

"I don't believe that he speaks English, Ma'am," said the nurse, who then translated the lady's words to Domingo. Domingo smiled softly and reached up to take the lady's hand. He said, "Your baby must have an angel watching out for him just like I do."

The nurse repeated Domingo's words in English to the lady and a small tear began to slide down the lady's cheek. "Please, nurse, ask him who he is and what can I ever do to repay him," she said.

The nurse asked him the lady's question. Domingo thought for a moment and then told his story of coming to America to find work to make money for his family and his village. He spoke of his dream and his angel and his disappointment that he could find no work and would make no money, and that now the Federals would surely send him back to Mexico.

"He is wet … an illegal alien, Ma'am," said the nurse, who went on to repeat Domingo's words.

When she had finished, the white lady spoke passionately, "You tell this boy that he most assuredly will not just be sent back to Mexico. I will see to that. I will sponsor him or whatever he wants." She trailed off and was lost in thought for several minutes. "Tell him, please, nurse," said the lady, after a long silence, "that my husband is the pastor of the Church of the Good Shepherd here in San Trejos. I have been discussing having our church sponsor a family in Mexico and it looks as though the Lord has brought one to us. Tell him that we will take up a collection of food, clothes, medicine, money, and whatever else we can get. When he and I are both well enough to travel, we will load all of it in my husband's pickup and drive it down to his village."

Now, it was the nurse's turn to be moved. The lady was going to fulfill the boy's dream, and it was almost as if the Savior himself had guided them to be together. "You are very kind and generous, and I know that you are going to make this child very happy," she said, lapsing into Spanish with her own happiness.

As the nurse spoke the lady's words to Domingo, a great big beaming smile broke out on his face, and he reached up for the lady's hand and kissed it. His dream was real. He had succeeded just when he thought all was lost.

The lady bent down and kissed Domingo on the forehead, and as she stood back up, she sagged a little. The nurse caught her by the shoulders and said, "You really should get some rest, you have been through much."

"You are right, of course, nurse, I must get well, and he must get well. But, one more thing: ask him what his name is, please."

"His name is Domingo. It means Sunday in English," answered the nurse.

"Sunday, hmmm, the Lord's Day. That is somehow very fitting," said the lady. "Tell him that the first Sunday he and I are both well, we will go to our church and tell everybody about the great miracle that has happened."

The nurse turned to Domingo to tell him, but he had fallen fast asleep. The nurse put her arm around the lady to support her and led her out the door. Domingo, of course, was dreaming. But this time, his dream was more than just a dream of hope.

瀞 "Buddy"
Texas

I sought the LORD, and he heard me, and delivered me from all my fears.

Psalm 34:4

Angels of Love and World Peace

*Put your brushes down. You are to paint
with your fingertips and hands.*

I've always believed in God and angels, and I've always considered myself to be spiritual and a child of God, as we all are. I was raised Catholic in Cleveland, Ohio, in the 50s, and I grew up with strict Roman Catholic rules. We were expected to attend church every Sunday and every holy day. Considering we'd have to answer to the priests in the confessional, we didn't dare miss Mass. Don't get me wrong. As I said, I believe in God, and I feel I've had several wake-up calls. I firmly believe that the universe has given me signs, even as a child, regarding what path I'd be on. Imagine having neighbors with the last name "Apostle."

My first wake up call was in 1980, when, after just returning from my honeymoon, I was almost killed by a drunk on the Cleveland Shore Way. My husband and I were hit from behind and were thrown, spinning over one hundred feet along the cement barrier and ending up facing oncoming traffic. Everyone said there was no way we should have survived that crash. I knew then that someone somewhere was watching over me. If I could survive that crash, a crash that left our car looking like an accordion, I knew that God had to have plans for me. I just didn't know what they were at the time.

Forgiveness was definitely one of the things I would learn from that experience. When I forgave the man who almost took my life, I started to heal fast. If I had made the choice to stay angry all these years, I'd probably be in a wheelchair. This has certainly been an important lesson to pass on to others in my life. Perhaps life is "earth school," where we all come to learn or teach lessons. I can testify that I am celebrating my thirtieth anniversary, and I'm now a life coach, helping others to perceive their difficult situations differently. I've coached over three thousand people, so the reason I had that car accident makes sense now. Your mind is more powerful than you realize.

In 1984, we moved to Connecticut, and I started a business painting town greens the way they appeared in the 1800s, complete with horse-drawn buggies. One day, in the middle of filling an order for a shop in New England, I heard a voice whose message was crystal clear, even though I heard it telepathically: "The order you are working on is not important!" *Well*, I thought, *I just didn't get enough sleep last night.* I continued on framing. Again, I heard, "The order you are working on is not important!"

Soon after, that same morning, the phone rang. It was the owner of that shop, telling me how she had to cancel this order because she had lost her lease. The order really was *not* important!

The next voice that came through told me to go outside to the woods and paint an angel. The energy was so intense that it felt like someone was pushing me out of the house and into my backyard.

So, I sat there in front of a blank canvas with my paintbrushes. I heard, "Put your brushes down. You are to paint with your fingertips and hands. The energy will come through your fingertips."

What transpired on canvas that day left me speechless. Creating this piece with my bare hands and whatever nature provided was truly amazing. I asked God for a sign because, quite frankly, I had no idea what the heck I was doing. For ten years, I had painted with brush tips the size of an eyeliner brush to get the detail I was known for. When I asked for this sign, the most beautiful iridescent dragonfly landed on the upper left corner of the painting and just sat there for two or three minutes. To this day, I've never seen another like it. It was a luminous teal green, and it was much larger than any I've ever seen.

By sunset, the entire piece was finished, and it brought me to tears. I was later told the name of the angel who guided me that day was Gladys. A woman who had a sister named Gladys who was going through a difficult situation in her life later purchased this painting.

I had been given many messages throughout the course of painting these ethereal messengers of light, such as "Your work must reflect the light!"

The bottom line was that we humans make things so complicated and that *love* is what it's all about, treating others as you would have them treat you, because we are all connected. As I opened myself up to the angelic realm, I acknowledged their angels' presence and meditated daily. As I found my quiet space, more messages came through.

It was as if a whole side of me was being unlocked. *Nature Angel* came through and again was created using only the tools that nature provided. I made stars in the painting from "stamps" that I made by carving stars in the roots of plants. I collected mica from the earth and pieced it into the work or crushed it into fine dust to add to the painting to reflect the light. I later found out that mica was used by the Native Americans to open their spiritual paths.

World Peace Angel came out after I attended an "angel gathering" class in an angel shop that my friend Arlene owned in Milford, Connecticut. Angels Coffee and Tea Room (no longer there) had a special gathering of people who wanted to write to angels and get messages from them. It was after hours in this lovely shop, and there were about ten of us seated in a circle. We all asked our angels if there was anything they wanted us to know, and we all started to write.

When we were through, we went around the circle and read our messages. It turned out that everyone's messages had one common thread: world peace. The next morning, I took a blank canvas to the woods and began painting what would become *World Peace Angel*. This one took me longer than a day, and the detail that was coming out in front of me took my breath away. I knew then that this one was very special and was meant for great things.

One of the messages I received while painting this angel was that she *must* get out to the world. When I finished painting her, I ran across a saying that my friend in Cleveland, Ohio, had given me some twenty-five years prior. I knew immediately it was meant to be added to this angelic image. I had no idea who had written these lovely words, but the message said, "If there is righteousness in the heart, there will be beauty in the character. If there is beauty in the character, there will be order in the nation. When there is order in the nation, there will be peace in the world."

How simple these words are, yet how true. My angelic messengers then led me to the calligrapher and printer in Florida who worked with me to find inks that would reflect the light, the hardest part of this job! No, I'll take that back. The hardest part was finding a magazine to advertise prints of my painting in. I started calling national magazines daily and reeling from sticker shock when I was told the price to advertise it was $152,000 for a full-color page ad for one month. The next magazine quoted me $90,000 for a one-time ad. After a morning of these unbelievable quotes that I couldn't afford, I remember sitting on my living room floor and having a good cry. I said, "Look God! I did my part. I painted the Angel (*World Peace*), got her printed with the last of my meager savings, and I went into debt over this print job. There was no way I can afford to advertise her," I said. "God, *please* send me an angel!"

At that point, I lost it and cried even harder, thinking *I must be crazy to be doing all this, let alone risking my finances. What would my husband think?* I remember lying on the floor in the living room, sobbing my eyes out. Of course, it didn't help that my husband was very irritated with me that morning when he left for work because I had just emptied my savings account to pay for the lithographs and now had no money to work with. I can only imagine what was going on in his head at the time: "This is not the girl I married!"

The next thing I remember, and I was fully awake because it was around 9:00 a.m., was that I sat up, still on the living room floor, and turned around. There, against my living room wall, was an incredible "light being." There were no pictures hanging on our wall at the time, as we had just finished painting it a tan color and hadn't re-hung anything yet. As I sat up, I propped myself up against the legs of a wing chair and stared in awe at this incredible image in beautiful white light standing before me. I knew I wasn't dreaming. I could plainly see the figure before me in pale white light. I could see the outline of a waist with a rope tie (almost like a monk's robe). The dress was long, but what mesmerized me were the arms that were extended as if this being was bending toward me to hand me the ball of light it was holding. The arms went from a soft faint light to continually brighter and lighter. The ball of light was a soft gray that kept pulsating, and as it did, it got lighter and whiter. It was as if the angel were handing me the ball. I remember feeling overwhelmed with the peace and love that it relayed to me, "Don't worry, I am with you. We are all here with you to help."

I saw energy coming from what we would normally call wings. This light was soft, but it moved ever so slowly. The arms kept getting brighter in intensity, as did the ball of light the figure was carrying. I know that whoever this was, whatever this was, gave me incredible love, and there was a total peace that came over me. I just *knew* that everything would be okay.

Shortly after (within an hour or two), I got a telephone call from one of the magazines I had called previously, and the gentleman said they had an inside cover space open up and were in a tight squeeze for this press date, the Christmas issue! He said he'd only charge me $1,500 with three months to pay! I couldn't speak because I was trying to digest it all, but realizing I didn't even have fifteen cents, I waited for the person to speak. He said, "Not to worry. We'll go ahead and bill you after it runs with no money down!" So without one red cent, *World Peace Angel* got into a national magazine's largest issue. Letters and calls came in from around the nation, with many telling me their own angel stories and about how they were touched by my celestial creation. The angels had kept their promise to help me, and I'm convinced that God *did* send an angel!

There are countless stories, too many to list here, but one of the things I heard via these messengers was that my work would be seen by millions and that many world leaders would receive my paintings. I remember calling the United Nations one fall morning and getting rejected by the gift shop there. They said they only carried items with the UN logo on it and told me they would not carry anything related to angels, as selling religious items may offend some people!

Again, I heard the voice I had heard so many times before saying, "You have the power of the universe behind you! Now call them right back!"

I got right back on the telephone to the UN, and after getting rerouted many times, I spoke with a young woman there. I told her what I had created and that I'd like to donate this World Peace Angel print to the UN. She couldn't have been nicer and told me where to mail it.

Time went by, and I heard nothing. I left for a trip to Florida to hear some best-selling angel authors, and on my return, I found an envelope sitting in my mailbox marked "official business, the United Nations" and hand-addressed to me. I opened it up and almost fell over. It was a personal, handwritten note from Madeleine Albright, thanking me for this donation. The Chief of Protocol somehow presented my print to her. She hung it on the outside of her office wall for all the world and visitors to see.

Many things happened after that. I was invited to the UN to present *World Peace Angel* to the former president of Costa Rica in front of many peacemakers. This former president backed me up in front of the group, saying that he could not do his world peace work without his "legions of angels behind him!" How awesome was that?

I was then asked by the president of the World Citizen Diplomats to be the director of the International Angels for World Peace, a non-governmental organization (NGO). Weeks later, my then fourteen-year-old son, Christopher, left a phone message for me at home from a Lorraine at "Lighthouse Gifts," saying that I should call her back. When I did, she said, "No, no, this is the White House!" (So much for my teenage son taking messages!) A *World Peace Angel* print was then sent to the White House.

One more thing … my son Christopher came home from school one day to tell me that they were learning philosophy. "Guess what, Mom? I know who wrote your peace message on your print! Confucius, 400 BC!"

ॐ Joanne Macko
Illinois

Bless the Lord, ye his angels, that excel in strength, that do his commandments, hearkening unto the voice of his word.

Psalm 103:20

Note

Joanne continues to sell her angelic creations worldwide and has had representatives in Japan for the last eight years. Her *World Peace Angel* print was just presented to His Holiness the Dalai Lama on his seventy-fifth birthday by a representative of the Tibetan Youth Council on June 6, 2010. Joanne also produces an annual event called "Lightworkers Midwest Conference" to unite people from around the world to help move humanity forward.

www.lightworkersconference.com

If you'd like to see Joanne's angel paintings, you can view them on her website:

www.angelic-art.com

Reflections of Love

As I stared into the mirror, I heard a voice.
"You are sweet and beautiful in the
eyes of God, who made you."

Every morning I repeated the same ritual. I waited until my husband left for work and for the house to become a quiet and solemn retreat, and then I showered. I tried to wash the pain away and prepare to face another day. The hot water peppered my body and raced down the drain, taking with it all the last vestiges of sleep. I felt good … as good as I was likely to feel all day, and I wished I could keep that feeling in a tiny flask around my neck to use as the day wore on.

I stepped out of the shower and began to towel myself dry: first my long dark hair, then my arms, legs, and belly, and finally, my feet and back. Then I looked into the mirror on the bathroom wall and stared at the reflection there. I saw myself in the worst possible light, naked and quivering, and the negative thoughts began to crown my mind. "I am so fat," I moaned. I examined the stretch marks on my upper legs and breasts. I counted the flat brown moles that covered my back … all eleven of them. I turned slightly to one side and noticed that my stomach protruded just enough to counterbalance my buttocks in the back, as if less in either place would cause me to topple over. I shook my body just a little and watched the ripple of flesh as it jiggled in every part of my torso. Feelings of unworthiness and pain filled my mind. It was the same every single day, this ritual. I would examine every imperfection and grieve for my loss of youth. I would criticize each part of myself harshly. I would often cry for a while, and then I would begin to make promises to myself. *Today, I will not eat anything that will make me fat. Today, I will exercise. Today, I will give up cream in my coffee and butter on my toast. Today will be the first day of the rest of my life, and I will change just like a beautiful butterfly.*

Unfortunately, every day played over and over like an old record, because once I had dressed and gone downstairs, my emotions were somersaulting with criticism and abuse. These feelings guided me to the kitchen, where I would find the only solace I had ever known. Promises made became promises broken, but the food tasted so good. I knew that I would pay the price later, but for the moment, I just ate. Usually, this was the next part of my daily ritual—usually.

Today played a little differently, though, as I glanced back into the mirror just before I was to get dressed. I noticed a distinct gray halo surrounding my entire body. I turned to face the mirror to look more closely. Yes, there was a definite gray shadow about three inches thick, and it encased my silhouette entirely. As I stared into the mirror, I heard a voice: "You are sweet and beautiful in the eyes of God, who made you. Your shape makes no difference to those who love you. You are perfection, a body full of light and love. Stop this self-destruction now before it ruins your entire life."

I was stunned, but I could not deny that the voice was real, for it was clear and distinct and echoed about the ceramic bathroom. A vision appeared in the mirror just above and to the left of my reflection … the face of an angel … a face I instantly recognized from many of my dreams. The angel face smiled, and her eyes swept over my naked body. There was no reaction or revulsion; only love poured forth from her face. The angel spoke once more, "Look carefully into the mirror, and tell me, what do you see?"

I looked long and hard before replying, "I see my overweight and imperfect body, and I am surrounded by a gray layer of something."

The angel looked at me with eyes of love and responded, "The gray halo is one of your own making, dear. Would you like to see what I see when I look at you each morning? Would you like to see what God sees?

I nodded and watched as the reflection changed before my eyes. Where an overweight naked woman had been reflected in the mirror was now a sphere of shining light. The light played and danced over the surface of the mirror and broke into crystals of rainbow-colored hues. I could no longer see my features. There was no body and no face, just a dazzling shape filled with sparkling lights. I was overwhelmed with the beauty that was reflected there, and I began to appreciate every aspect of this vision. The gray halo changed to a blue-white light radiating from the outline in the mirror.

The angel then smiled and said, "Dear Susan, you have seen yourself in the truest light, and you have finally changed your halo to one that matches your spirit. Keep those thoughts close to your heart, and live your life in peace. You may or may not change your outer characteristics, but know that whatever you do, you cannot change the perfection that dwells within."

I was stunned. As I continued to look at the vision in the mirror, I saw that my body was slowly coming back into focus. For the first time in my life, I saw my body as beautiful, and the halo surrounding me remained a stunning blue-white light.

A healing had taken place that morning. I had always been so hard on myself. I saw the beauty inside for the very first time, and I then became beautiful on the outside, too, even though I hadn't changed my physical self at all.

೪ Susan
Colorado

For the Lord seeth not as man seeth; for man looketh on the outward appearance, but the Lord looketh on the heart.

1 Samuel 16:7

THE MIRACLE OF THE TWISTED VINE

I saw my life flash before my eyes …
everything and everyone who was important
to me was in a flash of light.

It was New Year's Eve, and I was driving home from work. It was a beautiful sunny day. I was not rushed, just enjoying the drive, so I decided to drive on some back roads before I got on the highway. The traffic was light, as it was only about 2:00 in the afternoon.

I hadn't been on the highway more than about a mile or so when the steering wheel seemed to pull toward the left. I thought to myself, *That's strange,* and turned the wheel in the opposite direction so that I wouldn't hit the concrete barrier dividing the highway. When I turned the wheel, something snapped, and I lost complete control of the car. I tried to step on the brakes, but couldn't. The car crossed over the right lane and shoulder and traveled down a steep 120-foot embankment toward some railroad tracks at the end. There were a lot of small trees and brush in the car's path. I couldn't stop! I saw my life flash before my eyes … everything and everyone who was important to me was in a flash of light. Everything from when I was a little girl to the present was in my vision, it seemed. I kept on thinking that I was not going to live. I was so scared! *I am not ready to go yet! I am only twenty-three years old! No!*

All of a sudden, the car stopped abruptly, about twenty-five feet before the railroad tracks. I looked down at my feet, thinking that they were on the brakes, but the power of the car losing control had forced my feet to the left of the brake pedal. I looked around to make sure I was really seeing that the car had stopped, as I was a little disoriented. As soon as I realized that it was true, I grabbed my keys out of the ignition and my purse and got out of the car.

I started walking up the steep hill toward the highway to get help. There were some houses on the other side of the highway, where I thought I would stop to call for help. I was sure that someone would let me use a telephone. I looked back at the car and was in awe that it had stopped suddenly the way it did and that I was walking away from it, so far appearing to have no injuries.

Wondering how it happened and how the car had stopped, I realized that I must have had angels with me in this freak accident. God had been with me, there was no other explanation. When I turned back toward the highway and continued walking up the hill, I saw a car pull up and stop on the side of the road and wait for me. When I reached the car, the two people inside told me that they had been traveling in the opposite direction on the highway and had seen me lose control. They had turned around at the first place they could and had driven to the site where my car went down the embankment. They told me that they were a married couple and that they were just coming from the city I was driving to. They did not hesitate to offer me a ride home, even though it was at least twenty miles out of their way. On the way to my house, they told me all that they had seen and said that I was probably in shock. They left after they made sure I was okay at home and after they offered to stay with me until someone else arrived.

Later, my family and I went to look at the car to see what could possibly have happened. Of course, this was after hours on New Year's Eve, so there were no tow trucks available until the next day. While there at the site, we gathered my belongings from the car and tried to figure out what could have happened. There was no apparent answer ... until I saw something intriguing: it was a vine that was wrapped all the way around the car. It was a tiny twist of branches, brown and dried from the January cold. *Could this be the reason the car stopped?* I wondered to myself. I kept it to myself for a long time and considered myself blessed by God.

After the car was towed (they had to winch the car out using chains and all), we identified that a defective tie-rod had caused my loss of control of the steering column. The men who winched the car out of the bottom of the embankment said to me that they could not see any reason for this car to have stopped the way it did. That tiny vine could not have stopped a car going fifty-five miles per hour down a steep hill. I know how it did! It was God and His miracle helpers that we call angels. Now, years later, I look at the pictures and see that tiny twisted vine and know that I was saved by the angels and blessed by God.

& Julie
South Dakota

Fear thou not; for I am with thee: be not dismayed; for I am thy God: I will strengthen thee; yea, I will help thee; yea, I will uphold thee with the right hand of my righteousness.

Isaiah 41:10

Secret Service Angel

I lay there motionless, listening intently to the sounds of the crackling of static electricity and the unfolding of feathers!

*O*utside, a hazy moon hid behind dark clouds and mingled with the dense fog. This fog rolls in nightly over a high mountain range that hides the vast expanse of the Pacific Ocean. It was an unusually dark night about a week before the fires broke out in the Oakland-Berkeley Hills and caused millions of dollars of damage to the area's beautiful homes. Dillon, our four-year-old son, desiring a sense of security, climbed into bed between my husband and me and quickly drifted off to sleep.

Exhausted from a hectic workweek with hour-long commutes, we wearily resisted the usual response to get up, turn on a nightlight, and carry Dillon off to his bed. Instead, we effortlessly followed his cue and drifted off to sleep. Sometime in the middle of the night, I was awakened, gripped by an unusual sense of fear. Without moonlight streaming through our Venetian blinds and without any nightlights, the room appeared particularly dark. Instinctively, I became aware of an evil presence on the left side of my bed.

As I turned my head to take a look, I was startled by unusually strange sounds occurring simultaneously on my right side. My brave attempt to view the presence on my left was quickly aborted by fear. I lay there motionless, listening intently to the sounds of the crackling of static electricity and the unfolding of feathers!

To my utter amazement and wonder, I saw a youthful being sitting up in bed right next to me (where Dillon had been sleeping), looking straight ahead. From my position, I couldn't see the being's face, but I studied it from the backside, waist up. The being was Caucasian and had neck length, blonde hair and a long white robe with a cummerbund type of sash around its waist. Strangely enough, I didn't see any wings to account for the sounds of unfolding feathers that I had heard. Unafraid, I wondered who this being was and how he got into our bed.

Suddenly, without a sound, the being was in the air, hovering over our bed. He was looking at the floor area between the left side of the bed and the outer wall where the presence of an evil entity had been detected. Although no words were exchanged between us, somehow the being seemed to know exactly where to look!

Viewing the being from this vantage point, I realized that for the first time in my life, I was actually looking at a real angel! The being appeared to be a handsome, youthful male between the ages of eighteen and twenty-five, and he had an authoritative, challenging look on his face.

The angel scowled as he glared intently at the evil entity as if to say, "What do you think you're doing here? Get out *now*!" He obviously did not approve of what he was seeing! Though no words were spoken, his expression more than adequately conveyed his thoughts.

Fascinated by the apparent standoff between the angel and the evil entity, my eyes remained fixed on this incredible being. Consequently, I never satisfied my curiosity to view what the evil entity looked like. The angelic being suddenly appeared on the floor at the foot of my bed and walked between my bed and dresser. At this point, I could no longer make out the angel's physical details. Instead, because of the distance and darkness, he appeared as an illuminated moving outline. It was like taking a piece of chalk and drawing a clear, bluish-white outline of an angel on a blackboard, except the outline moved about, and the outer lines of its image were lit like a soft neon or fluorescent light. Unlike halos depicted in Renaissance art around an angel's head, this "halo effect" surrounded the angel's entire body!

I watched with great interest while the angel darted back and forth as though he were jockeying for position to take on the evil entity in battle, or he may have already been engaged in battle at that point. Then, just as unexpectedly, the angel stopped jockeying back and forth. He took off and headed toward the left side of my bed in hot pursuit of the evil entity that had frightened me.

A few moments later, a sense of peace came over me. With an indication that everything was now okay, I no longer needed to fear and could go back so sleep. I smiled, closed my eyes, and didn't wake up again until early the next morning.

Being the first to wake up that morning, I instantly became aware that something incredible had occurred during the night. I suddenly remembered the nighttime encounter.

Quickly, I turned my head to my right and was reassured to see Dillon sound asleep between my husband and me, right where I had seen the supernatural visitor the night before.

Before getting out of bed, I woke both Dillon and my husband to tell them I had seen an angel during the night. They looked at me somewhat incredulously. When I told Dillon I suspected it was his guardian angel, an unforgettable wide grin spread across his face.

As I recalled the night's incredible encounter, I was filled with what could only be described as a supernatural wonder, a wonder similar to what the shepherds in Bethlehem must have felt when their serene reality was suddenly jolted by the presence of supernatural beings from another dimension. Their dark night skies burst alive, ablaze with ethereal bright lights, colors, and sounds. Then the beings made the most incredible announcement in human history—the arrival of Immanuel, meaning "God with us," disguised in the unsuspecting form of a newborn baby. My feeling of awe and supernatural wonder was heightened by an unusual, effervescent kind of joy and peace, which lasted about a month afterward.

I have never heard of angels lying in bed with humans as they slept! However, the Bible does say, "The angel of the Lord *encampeth* round about them that fear him, and delivereth them." (Psalm 34:7). It also says that children's angels "always behold the face of my Father" (Matthew 18:10). I interpret this to mean that children's angels have unrestricted and immediate access to God for help in matters of urgency, since children aren't as capable of helping themselves as adults are.

I'd been visited by these evil entities in the night before, when Dillon wasn't with me, and I'd had only my cries to God for help to fight them off. Notably, Dillon has always been quick to come to my aid in times of distress. Therefore, since we were all together in bed, totally vulnerable in our sleeping state, it isn't surprising that his angel would be alerted and bring immediate help from God.

Some may ask why God permitted me to view this unusual battle between two supernatural beings. I believe God was affirming that He hears my prayers every night for protection. By opening my physical eyes to see into the spiritual realm (giving me a vision), God enabled me to view the activities of one of His active, on-duty "secret service agents," confirming that my prayers weren't just monotonous, repetitive nightly recitations. Rather, my prayers were valid concerns that He deemed important. Interestingly enough, the evil entities have not returned since that encounter.

ॐ Stacy
California

I will both lay me down in peace, and sleep: for thou, Lord, only makest me dwell in safety.

Psalm 4:8

Help from a Stranger

*When we turned around, we saw that they both had
what looked like huge knives in their hands.*

I was around thirteen years of age when a friend and I
agreed to house-sit for a family in Wisconsin. Being
teenagers, we stayed up late and started getting hungry for
a very late night snack. It was about three in the morning
when we decided that we were hungry for Pop-Tarts. We
decided to wander off and see if we could find an open store,
but we had no luck finding any stores open at that late hour.
We were at least fifteen or twenty blocks from the house
when we noticed two men following a little bit behind us.

We started walking faster, and so did they. When we turned
around, we saw that they both had what looked like huge
knives in their hands. One of them moved toward us. We
were about to be cornered. We were looking for lights on
in the surrounding houses or an open gas station, but there
was nothing. We were completely trapped, and there was
nobody around.

It was strange, because we were very aware of our surroundings
and were looking for help, but the streets were totally vacant.

Then a station wagon that seemed to come from nowhere pulled up to us and stopped. There was a very tall man who appeared to be about twenty years old at the wheel. He had the kindest and calmest face. He just whispered to us, "Those people are going to hurt you. Get into the car."

So, we did as we were told. It wasn't really like us to get into a car with a stranger, yet we were really in danger and didn't think much of it at the time. We didn't tell him where we were going, as we were so shaken up. We were astonished when we saw where he brought us. He had driven us to the front door of the house we were house-sitting! He said, "You'll be okay now; be careful."

We said, "Thanks," but somehow that was all we could say. We were still very scared and upset.

A couple of days later, we heard of a woman who had been hurt by two men in the same area, but she also got away. The police found and arrested the attackers later that week. When we look back on that day, we know God was protecting us. He sent a protector, whom we feel was a guardian angel, to help us back home to safety.

&❧ Carrie
Wisconsin

Be not forgetful to entertain strangers; for thereby some have entertained angels unawares.

Hebrews 13:2

ON THE EDGE OF ETERNITY

I knew this voice. It was filled with and radiated compassion, a love that encompassed and filled me. It was so breathtakingly beautiful that even more tears filled my eyes.

*D*idn't you just want to sit on a cloud or be able to fly when you were a kid? I did. Oh, I did! My eyes were always upward, just waiting for a cloud to come down and pick me up. Well, years later, I got my wish. It would take three near-death experiences for me to find this wondrous, glorious, light cloud … but I would, and I did. It wasn't my choice; it was the Divine's intervention into my existence. My life would be forever changed, and profoundly!

My experience began after going through some extremely difficult tests. I was diagnosed with a diseased gall bladder and was sicker than any of my doctors ever knew. At one point, one of my doctors had to go to my primary care doctor so that I could be sent to the emergency room. Then, after my nurse practitioner and the doctor conferred back and forth, in and out of my room, they finally decided to just send me back home. I was doubled over with pain, and they decided to send me home … without pain medication!

Back home, back in bed (I had been bedridden for two months at this point), my eyesight was diminishing and my pain was intensifying. An earthly tiredness began to blanket me, pulling me down and down even deeper until I felt a part of the earth. It was a chore to even lift my finger, and my strength to fight for life was filtering out of me. I was just too tired to fight anymore.

As I started to fade away, pictures of each of my family members began to flash before me with feelings that I had been such a drain on them. Tears began gently streaming down my face. I felt that perhaps they would be better off without me. That's when I heard a voice audibly speak my name, "Lindell."

I knew this voice. It was filled with and radiated compassion, a love that encompassed and filled me. It was so breathtakingly beautiful that even more tears filled my eyes. This voice told me that it was all right if I wanted to let go … and I did!

It was then that I heard the music. This music was alive, filled with this same love. It comforted me completely. The only way I can describe it is like this: Have you ever seen the photos taken from the Hubble Space Telescope? The ones documenting the birth of a star? This music seemed to embody something similarly magnificent, celestial, and eternal. It spoke of the planets, the stars, and the angels. It was composed of voices and instruments—bells, birds, and things I cannot identify … things celestial. It was so beautiful, so beautiful and alive, and totally filled with love. It comforted me completely.

While all this was being played out, something drew my attention to the end of my bed, where a smoky, foggy mist was forming. The closer it came to me, the farther I felt from myself, my room, and this earth. Then, quicker than a blink, I found myself standing in a cloud-like tunnel that was slowly revolving clockwise around me. I was filled with joy and such ecstasy! I was so happy! It was beautiful and fascinating, heavenly and sacred, all at the same time. All was bathed in this radiant pure white light. I just stood there, mesmerized by the way the light danced with the most alive, pastel colors I had ever seen. They seemed to sparkle and shine like glitter or like thousands and thousands of lights, as small as sand. Something drew me to the center of this fascinating place, this cloud-like tunnel, to where the source of all the light was coming from. It was an intense bright light that seemed to be translucent and alive, filled with unconditional love. This love was all encompassing. Somehow, I knew this love. I knew that this was where I had come from. This was home; I was home. I was home, and I never wanted to leave.

Then up and out of the light came a figure. I believe it was Jesus, and light refracted off Him like splinters from mirrored glass. I saw the side of His cheek, and His hands outstretched to receive me.

My phone started ringing next to my bed, bringing me back to my room, where the misty fog still hung and music still played. My friend had become worried about me and decided to call. She said that I sounded hollow, like I was in a cave very far away. A few more days passed, and again this experience repeated itself—right down to my friend calling me.

On the day of my gall bladder surgery, my spirits rallied. I shared my miraculous experience with a pastor, who was in the surgical waiting room. He was so moved by this experience, he left shaking my hand with teary eyes. Then a nurse who also listened in was so inspired that she just hugged me and said, "God's going to use you, girl! He's going to use you in a mighty way!" Deep in my own heart, I felt it, too. The miracles were yet to come.

There wasn't time to think about what had taken place, being so very ill and with surgery coming so soon. My sights were set on getting through the surgery. Almost five hours later (normal surgery for a gall bladder is about one and a half hours), I was being wheeled to my room. Three days later, I was on my way home. Unknowingly, I was facing two more months of being bedridden and almost four years of crawling my way back toward health.

My surgeon, while shaking his head in amazement at my six-week checkup, stated that he didn't know how I had made it so far, because of how sick I had been up to this point! Months later, I was still not better. It felt as though I still had one foot in heaven and one foot on earth—as though I was in the valley of choice.

At a friend's house, my friend asked if she and some other women could pray for me because I looked so ill. I told them that I would take all the prayer I could get! So, as they began to audibly pray for me, I settled back in the soft chair, leaning my head back in relaxation. At that moment, somehow I was lifted out of my body and found myself standing in heaven, barefoot, on a green, lush, grassy hill that overlooked a valley with no shadow in it. This grass was alive and buoyant, holding me up. I could distinctly feel each blade under my feet, giving me life. Oh, and the music! The same music that had filled my room was there: bells, birds, voices, instruments, and the music of the spheres: the melody of heaven.

The flowers emitted light and life, vibrantly alive with color, and everything was at the very peak of perfection. The sky was an azure/sapphire blue and the breeze blanketed me, soothing away all my worries and sorrows, healing my wounds, and then leaving only to come back again and again.

I began to hear people gathering behind me, and as I turned to look, bounding before me in white letters came the prayers of my friends. I not only saw their prayers, but also heard them in their own voices. The prayers rolled gently before me, caught me up with them, and then flung me back in my body with a thud so hard my hair flew up. Once back, I opened my eyes to see if they, my praying friends, had seen anything. I saw them huddled near me, eyes closed, still intent in prayer.

My whole world changed from that moment on. You cannot be touched by heaven and not be changed. I had been touched three times, profoundly. The Divine, for some reason, had reached down into this mere mortal's life and changed the course I was on.

After this experience, I had a voracious appetite to read and learn everything that I could get my hands on about what had happened to me. I liked to call these NDEs (near death experiences) or my NDAs (near death awakenings)! I read and read and read. I read all I could about Native Americans. The more I read, the more alarmed and appalled I felt at the outrageous and tragic atrocities my white race had forced upon them. I was ashamed and filled with deep sorrow. I then read about African Americans. I read actual slave accounts and the Underground Railroad, later watching the movie *Amistad*. Realizing the tremendous spirit within both the Native and African Americans was a powerful way for the Divine to use and mold me according to my purpose and to help me understand the importance of unconditional love.

The journey and quest of understanding began. The farther I walked, the more enlightenment began to flood my being. Instead of losing my love for Christ Jesus, I began to lose my ties to dogma and religion. My spirit, my soul, began to sprout wings, and this love born on the "wings of heaven" arose! It flooded my being, bringing out joy and creativity. It burst forth in angel art, cards, crafts, and in writing and speaking to others about my newfound knowledge.

Then wondrous new things began to happen. I began to see angels in my home and in the fields surrounding my home. I also began to see angels around others. They gave me messages for those sitting and visiting with me. They also began to give me messages about "the Light" and told me to remind everyone of who we really are. We are powerful, spiritual beings who have come *from* this Light. I began to be much more intuitive, opening my heart to more spiritual knowledge.

One thing I knew for sure was that the most important thing is love. I began making little homespun angel booklets by hand with messages of love. Tears would form in people's eyes as they read them, and by viewing the simple drawings. Their soul and spirit began opening up. They were remembering, you see, our true source. All of my artwork seemed to do one common thing: to connect the heart to the Divine, in love. It made my heart sing, for I heard the melody of heaven begin to play its song of remembrance within my soul and spirit. I was humbled that Divinity had stepped into their lives and mine so that this experience might come to pass. Their hearts were remembering the Divine connection, just like mine.

¨ Lindell
Michigan

The LORD is my shepherd; I shall not want. He maketh me to lie down in green pastures: he leadeth me beside the still waters. He restoreth my soul: he leadeth me in the paths of righteousness for his name's sake. Yea, though I walk through the valley of the shadow of death, I will fear no evil: for thou art with me; thy rod and thy staff they comfort me. Thou preparest a table before me in the presence of mine enemies: thou anointest my head with oil; my cup runneth over. Surely goodness and mercy shall follow me all the days of my life: and I will dwell in the house of the LORD for ever.

Psalm 23

JUST PASSING THROUGH

"You didn't make it, Sherry. I saw everything clearly, since I was directly behind you. You didn't make it, girl," she kept insisting.

This hard, cold winter had been unforgettable because of the vast amounts of snowfall and ice that had crippled our area for weeks. However, the beginning of March had given us promise of nicer weather. Spring slowly inched its way around the corner, and winter's worst temper tantrums gradually ceased, leaving only cold mornings, frost, and ice blanketing the vulnerable outdoors. Being a schoolteacher, I would leave early each morning for my twenty-minute drive to school. My youngest son, Justin, would accompany me, as he attended the same school. This time, to and from school, became a time of bonding throughout the years, creating precious memories between us.

That summer, we purchased another van; however, because of its extended top, we could not park it in our garage. On bitterly cold mornings, thick frost would form on my windows, forcing us to scrape each window before our departure. One ominous morning, as I was trying to scrape off a heavy coating of ice and frost, my husband appeared in the driveway with a kettle of hot, steaming water and threw it on the windshield of the van. Regardless of my alarm at the possible consequences of hot water on glass, he assured me the temperature was not that hot. As my wipers raced back and forth, the ice did magically vanish, but within seconds, ice crystallized once again across my windshield, leaving me frustrated.

My husband became perturbed and yelled for me to shut off the wipers, since he assumed they had caused the frost to reappear. He then departed only to reappear with more hot water. Upon his return, I reminded him that hot water froze faster than cold, which would account for the frost's quick return. Without heeding my warning, a surge of steaming water covered my windshield, and again the ice miraculously melted. "Don't turn your wipers on!" he admonished. So, slowly down the driveway, Justin and I ventured that dark, shivering-cold morning. As I carefully crept out onto our street toward the highway, a glaze of ice began to dance across my windshield; nevertheless, I still could slightly manage to see the road. I had lost valuable time and decided the defrosters would warm the glass by the time I hit the main road outside our subdivision.

Realizing my windshield was crystallizing, Justin asked if I could see. I replied "barely," and with the defrosters still on high, I switched on my wipers, hoping that the ice would dissipate faster. By then, I had slowly driven out onto the highway. To my horror, the condition worsened within seconds. The crystals became a thick opaque coat of milky white ice.

This time Justin screamed, "Mom, can you see?"

A "no" nervously groaned from my lips. Except for a tiny peephole at the bottom of the windshield where the wipers had rested seconds ago, I could not escape the blindness. With the realization of my circumstance, I began to tremble, knowing full well we were headed for trouble and that I must pull off the highway; however, I could not see the road. My speed had diminished to a crawl. I was aware that I also could not see traffic behind me, around me, or in front of me. Searching for any way to see, I discovered that I could see the highway's dividing line through the peephole that was still visible. Knowing my son's fear, I assured Justin that I was able to see the dividing line and that I'd try to find the shoulder of the road to pull over.

All of the sudden, Justin yelled, "Mom, look at the light!"

I, too, had looked up at that precarious moment and had seen through a glazed windshield a light so bright that it reminded me of train lights. Shaking, I screamed out to Justin, "My God, he's on our side of the highway!"

"No, Mom, I think you are on his side!" he blurted out in terror.

That thought raced through my mind as I was trying to figure out another answer, but he had to be right. The white line I had thought was the edge of the road was really the dividing line. By then, time slowed to a trickle. Aloud, I pleaded with God and my guardian angel to help me *immediately*! I needed help! A blaring startle of a horn intensified my fear. Dear God, it even sounded like a train. I knew that if I were in the wrong lane and tried to pull to the right, there might be a chance that I'd pull into the direct path of a car in the right lane. I only had a fraction of a second to make my choice. Slowly, hoping any cars in that lane could realize my dilemma and allow me in, I eased my van to the right lane.

My body stiffened as I whispered, "Spare my son, God, please spare my son!"

At that moment, a gush of wind rocked the van. Pebbles pelted its side. The lights that were upon us were overwhelming in brightness. Although the windows were up, a gush of wind passed through our vehicle. As our tires finally left the pavement and rolled slowly onto the shoulder, my body loosened, my muscles began to shake, and tears of thankfulness rolled down my cold cheeks. We were safe! I looked out to take a glimpse of what I had just missed only to see the black of the night staring me in the face. Whatever it was had passed us, and we had missed one another by millimeters, thank God. Safety embraced us again.

Justin looked over and noticed my exhausted condition. Since I was shaking so badly, I knew I wouldn't be able to drive for a while. Just then, I saw a car pulling up behind us as I glanced in my side mirror.

"Justin, I think an unmarked police car has just pulled up behind us. He probably witnessed the whole thing and thinks I'm drunk. I'll have to take a breath analysis test."

This was going to be embarrassing since I don't drink. I was also embarrassed to think he had witnessed my almost fatal accident, which would have been my fault. To the passenger side of our van came a pounding and familiar voice.

"Sherry, Sherry, are you alright?"

My neighbor, Diane, had pulled directly out behind me onto the highway and watched the nightmare unfold. She figured I had had a heart attack and watched in terror screaming from her window, "Get over, Sherry! Get over Sherry!" Finally, she realized I either couldn't hear her or wouldn't hear her in time. She also revealed that the vehicle that was upon us had been an eighteen-wheeler! As she questioned why I had been on "his" side of the road, I pointed to my windshield and explained briefly my error. Realizing I was in no condition to drive, she instructed me to remain in my van, and she would return shortly with my husband.

Later that evening, Diane called me to discuss once more my near death experience. At the end of our conversation, she explained that she had hesitated to call me; however, she wanted to relate to me what she had actually witnessed that I could not have because of the blinding ice.

"You didn't make it, Sherry. I saw everything clearly, since I was directly behind you. You didn't make it, girl," she kept insisting.

"I don't understand, Diane. I did make it! God must have heard my cry, or my guardian angel lost a few feathers on this one," I tried to jest.

"No, Sherry, I distinctly saw the left side of your van slowly pass through the left side of that truck as you tried pulling off the road. I could hardly believe what I was seeing, but I did see it. You didn't make it."

Stunned and speechless, I knew, too, that someone heard my cry that cold, dark morning and gave us another chance for life. Why? I don't know. I just know that there is someone watching over us. For years, I have believed in guardian angels. In fact, I named mine Constance long ago, since he is constantly watching over me.

෧ Sherry,
Ohio

He delivereth and rescueth, and he worketh signs
and wonders in heaven and in earth who hath
delivered Daniel from the power of the lions.

Daniel 6:27

Prayers Can Unlock Doors

I also know we all failed one of God's tests on patience and understanding that day, so I know we will be tested again in the future to see if we are learning our lessons in this life.

*M*y husband, two sons, and I had ventured off to a vacation that promised rest, relaxation, and freedom from work for just a short five days. We were determined to squeeze forty-eight hours into every twenty-four and yet return rested, with memories to fill a picture album. After loading the van Saturday evening, we returned to our beds to catch a few winks before our early morning escape to Florida. As my husband and I lay with excitement mounting, we glanced at each other, knowing what was in each other's hearts. Why not travel late at night, beating the heavy morning traffic and enjoying the refreshing coolness of the late night? It was early August; by 10:00 a.m., temperatures could already hit the mid-eighties.

Tense with adventure and our adrenaline pumping, we loaded up our sons and sneaked off into the darkness, a flight from the year's work pressures. We drove straight through Kentucky to Gulf Shores, Florida, with anticipation of a week of tranquility, frolicking along the ocean, and soft white sand to tickle our feet. Within fourteen hours, we would smell the ocean's breath, announcing that we had finally arrived.

On our fourth day, I decided that an excursion aboard a real naval aircraft carrier would be an educational and delightful break from the mystical daily pull of the gulf's white shores. Plus, I had been grounded from going out during the afternoon, thanks to a severe case of sunburn, my usual gift from Florida. Pensacola's famous USS Lexington was docked and offering guided tours. As we pulled into a parking space along the street, I decided to hide my purse under the seat, explaining to my husband that it would be one less thing to carry.

The sweltering heat had already begun to leave its mark on us, as tempers flared. Anxious to board the carrier, our sons leaped from the van as I was tucking my purse beneath my seat. "Don't forget the camcorder," I reminded my husband as he was about to pull the keys from the ignition. Instantly, he turned to the seat behind him, grabbed the camcorder, and hit the automatic lock button, securing the van's contents. As all locks simultaneously clicked and the final door slammed shut, a look of frustration crossed his face. "Honey, give me your keys. I forgot to pull them as I was getting the camcorder," he stated.

"Don't you remember? I told you, I was hiding my purse under the seat. They're in my purse," I replied.

As we all began pulling and tugging on the many stubborn doors of the van, we soon realized what a real predicament we faced.

My husband became the focal point of anger and blame. Trying to liberate himself from the mounting hostility, he announced that he would break one of the side windows to enable us to retrieve the dangling keys that were in clear view. I hastily interjected to give us another chance to recover the keys since a broken window would leave our van wide open for thieves.

My oldest son began angrily jerking the back door, even though my husband had previously tried breaking through the same door. Once again, fault was being tossed about like a ball. Seeing no other alternative, I walked to a pay phone a couple of blocks away to summon the city's police. A few years ago, I had locked my keys in our S-10 truck, and our local police had used a jimmy stick to finally unlock the door.

Within a few minutes, a patrol car drove by the deserted street. My sons and husband must have been a startling sight, as they were all banging and pulling on windows and doors still trying to break into the van. After a brief explanation of our plight, the police politely replied that it was against the law for them to use a jimmy stick, but they would be more than happy to drive me to my home for another set of keys. They did not realize that we were from Kentucky. Our only hope left was to wait a few hours for a locksmith to alleviate the frustrating mess.

The temperature was now hitting close to one hundred degrees, and so were tempers. Waiting was not going to be easy. Throughout the incident, I had forgotten to pray. Then, as if my guardian angel whispered into my ear, "Pray, Sarah," the message clicked, and I began to silently plead my case with my angel. I explained that this prayer needed answering soon. By then, the rage had developed into a battle of blame of which I had also become a victim.

With apprehension, I walked toward the back door of the van to pull the handle, expecting my miracle, when my sons and husband yelled out with irritation that they had already tried to budge the handle, but it stubbornly refused to open. "But

I asked my guardian angel's help," was all that tumbled from my mouth, hoping my angel would come to my rescue. Placing my fingertips inside the handle, and pausing briefly from fear of my prayer being turned down, I took a deep breath again and gingerly lifted the handle. Pop, went the door! I began to breathe again, as a wide grin ran across my face, and sweat continued to slide down my temples. *Yes! I was in!*

My hands trembled as my family flocked around the door. They meticulously examined it in bewilderment, asking me what I had done. They all had tried in vain to pry it open several times. With confidence, I announced, "It was my guardian angel. I told you I asked her to help us." Secretly, I was also in shock that my request had been granted.

One of my philosophies in life has been, "You have not, because you ask not." So, I ask. I am constantly asking for everything. The majority of the time, the answer is a big fat no, but when He finally says yes, I know it's time for me to receive my request. I also know we all failed one of God's tests on patience and understanding that day, so I know we will be tested again in the future to see if we are learning our lessons in this life. I hope I am passing this time. I'd hate to do this over again. I believe that life's lessons are doors to the soul's learning.

           ❧ Sarah
           Kentucky

For everyone that asketh receiveth; and he that seeketh findeth; and to him that knocketh it shall be opened.

Luke 11:10

THE MOUNTAIN ANGEL

I turned around to see who had helped me,
but there was no one around at all.

When I was sixteen years old, I was hiking on Lassen Peak in California with my church youth group. We were at the very top, walking along the trails. I found myself lagging behind everyone else, just enjoying the scenery.

When I came to a place in the trail that everyone else had passed, I went to cross over it as well. There was a sheer drop from where I was to the base of the mountain. I jumped across from one rock to land on another, when my foot slipped. At that same time, I felt someone grab my arm, which enabled me to land safely on the other side. I turned around to see who had helped me, but there was no one around at all.

I have never forgotten that experience, and I know in my heart that it was my guardian angel. He guides and protects me to this day.

As a nurse who works in home care, I drive every day to see my patients. The traffic is awful, and I have had many close misses that could have been serious accidents. I know my guardian angel is protecting me in my daily travels.

&❧ Kelly
California

For he shall give his angels charge over thee, to keep thee in all they ways. They shall bear thee up in their hands, lest thou dash thy foot against a stone.

Psalm 91:11-12

ANGEL BABY

*For years to come, I saw this little boy as plain as
day, just as I would if you and I met. One day when
he appeared, he said, "I will be born soon."*

When I was twelve, I had a dream. I was grown-up
and was in church attending a meeting. A child
came into the room and said, "Something bad has happened
downstairs." All the adults ran out of the meeting to the first
set of stairs, but I chose the second set of stairs down the
hall. When I got to the top of the stairs, there was a little
boy at the bottom looking up at me. He was about five or
six, with blonde hair, eyes as blue as the sky, blue knickers,
and saddle shoes. I started to run down the stairs, tripped,
and started to roll down them instead. Keeping my eyes on
him the whole way down to the bottom, I came to rest right
in front of him. I woke up instantly. I sat straight up in bed,
and the little boy was standing next to my bed. I asked him
what he wanted, and he said, "I want you to be my mommy."
I told him I was too young, and he said, "I will wait."

For years to come, I saw this little boy as plain as day, just as I would if you and I met. One day when he appeared, he said, "I will be born soon."

Two months later, I found out I was pregnant, and nine months later, I had a little boy I named Tommy. You see, the miraculous thing is that six months before I got pregnant, the doctors told me I would never have kids!

God loved me so much that He sent me my son! He sent him to me at the perfect time, when I needed him most in my life. He's changed my life in so many wonderful ways. My son, Tommy, is now four years old, and he still looks like that boy in my dreams. He will forever be my gift from heaven and my miracle "angel baby." Life is precious, and I can now say that I've been truly blessed.

Now, I see another angel. Her name is Aidia. She, as my son did, awaits her time to be born. My son sees her as well and says she is his "sissy." They "play together" and already they are close to each other. I look forward to the day God blesses me with Tommy's little sissy, my next little "angel baby."

❧ Bonnie
Kansas

Take heed that ye despise not one of these little ones; for I say unto you, That in heaven their angels do always behold the face of my Father which is in heaven.

Matthew 18:10

THE NURSE ANGEL

You are okay. God will take care of you. I am here now. You are not alone.

I remember that as a little girl, I used to tuck the angels who lay on my shoulders in bed at night. I used to talk to them and God about my day. I remember talking to them for hours. Then as I grew older, I forgot about God and the angels who protected me and were always there.

As I grew older, I grew depressed and started to cut myself as a way to get out of the pain. Then this practice grew into cutting myself to attempt suicide. I wanted to die. No one seemed to care about me or love me. I was put into a mental hospital just days after my seventeenth birthday. I went there to get some help, and they ended up keeping me there.

I met other kids like me, and we became friends. After I got out and started attending a Christian school, I received Jesus into my heart and was saved. Then, not long after that, I was put back into the hospital. What happened there changed my life.

I was really depressed as I lay in the hospital bed. Since I had tried to hurt myself, I was sleeping in the big room near the nurses' station. I hated it there, stuck in that hospital again! The room was dark other than the glow from the nurses' station. I could hear the staff being happy and laughing loudly. I curled up into a ball, crying as I continued to feel how badly my wrists hurt where I had cut them. As I cried, I began remembering all I had learned while in the Christian school. I knew God loved me and would take care of me, but I didn't understand why I was in this hospital again. I didn't want to be taken away from my parents again and shut away from the world. I hated having to ask permission to go to the bathroom and being put in time-outs like a two year old. All of these thoughts swirled in my head as I lay there.

As I continued to cry harder, I felt someone rubbing my back gently. I remembered what my friend Michelle, whom I had met there last time, had told me. She said that there was a nice late nurse who would sit with you sometimes. I rolled over to see her, and no one was there. I rolled over again, crying harder.

The hand came back, and a voice said into my ear, "It's okay, no one will hurt you ever again. Things will be different now. You are okay. You will get help here and be out soon."

I rolled over again to see who it was and noticed a glow in the corner of the room. I put on my glasses and still saw it, but it was impossible for light to be there. The nurses' station was far away from that corner of the room, and from its location, I knew it couldn't be car lights. I took off my glasses and lay back down, still crying. *I'm crazy*, I told myself.

"You are going to be fine," a voice said gently, and I felt warm arms all around me, holding me close. "You are okay. God will take care of you. I am here now. You are not alone."

Feeling suddenly calm and at peace, I drifted off to sleep.

A week later, I was out of the hospital. One day, at school in Bible class, a boy turned around to face me. "Why did you do that?" he said. "Why did you try to kill yourself?" I didn't answer. "My mom killed herself after I was born," he said, turning back around. His words changed my life that day. I realized that if I killed myself, I would be cheating my child to be, my husband to be, and other people's lives I was supposed to touch yet in this lifetime.

Years later, I met a wonderful man. He got me to go back to church, and we married. Now, at age twenty-one, I am blessed with a wonderful child, a little girl who is now six months old, whom we named Faith. One night soon after we got married, a show about angels came on television. What had happened to me years ago in that hospital suddenly hit me.

Now, when I can't sleep at night or I'm scared or upset, I can feel comforting arms around me. I know my angels are always there, sent by God to help me, guide me, and watch over me.

                                     ❧ Alicia,
                                        Georgia

In my distress I called upon the LORD, and cried
unto my God: he heard my voice out of his temple,
and my cry came before him, even into his ears.

Psalm 18:6

Angel Voices

*My body was no longer trembling from
sobbing. I was at total peace.*

*I wasn't afraid, I wasn't angry—I wasn't
anything for that moment.*

*I*t was Sunday evening, and I was doing a self-breast
examination as I took my shower. Never before had
I done this, and to this day, I still question what made me
do an examination that day. The only answer I have is that
my higher power, whom I prefer to call God, directed me
to do it without me realizing it. Upon examining my left
breast, I discovered a lump about the size of a marble. I
began examining my right breast, hoping to find the same
lump on the opposite side. But no, there was no lump in the
right breast. I felt the left breast again, hoping it was gone
and that I hadn't felt anything. The lump was still there in
the same position.

The next morning, I went into my doctor's office. I asked
to be examined and told her that I had discovered a lump.
My doctor told me it was nothing to worry about, that I
was twenty-nine years old, with no history of cancer in my

family, I didn't smoke, and I wasn't on the birth control pill. She sent me home and told me that I was fine. Unfortunately, I believed her. I didn't go to another doctor, but I now know that I should have.

About a week later, I phoned the same doctor and asked to be seen again. I explained that the lump was still there, only bigger. She more or less patronized me and said, "If it would make you feel better, than come in." Yes, it did make me feel better, so I went in, and this time my husband came along with me! After hearing the doctor say again that everything was fine, my husband asked that I have a mammogram done. The doctor ordered a mammogram, but unfortunately it was scheduled for two weeks away. I would have to wait and worry for two more weeks. Plus, the lump would continue to grow.

Again, we should have done something about the delay, but we had put our trust in the doctors once again. I had the mammogram done when the two weeks were up. When the results came in, I was told I would have to have a biopsy immediately.

I found a wonderful surgeon, and the surgery was scheduled for the next day. My surgeon was a wonderful, kind, and caring man. He tried to set my fears at ease by reminding me that I was only twenty-nine years old, had no history of cancer, and didn't smoke. He told me everything would be fine, but when I awoke after surgery, everything was *not* fine. I had cancer! My whole world felt like it was coming to an end. How could this be? How could I have cancer? I didn't smoke. My husband was the smoker. As strange as it sounds now, I was mad at the time that I had the cancer and that he didn't. I was a mommy. All I had ever dreamed of was being a mommy, and now, after two short years, it was all going to be taken away from me. No way! No way!

My doctor went over all my options and explained the procedures. He sent me home and told me to think things over. He asked me to think about the recommended procedures and decide which one would be best for me. Did I want to choose chemo and radiation, or a mastectomy and radiation? I was told that a fifteen-year study showed that one was not better than the other.

Four days after I was told that I had cancer, I found myself sitting in the middle of the bathroom floor, crying. That was where I could pour my heart out and let out all the fear and pain bottled up inside me without my family seeing my "weakness." My husband was asleep, as was the rest of my family. I had been so brave up to that point, so I couldn't let my family see that I was falling apart! I sat there and cried, fearing the worst and the unknown. All of a sudden, I heard the most beautiful music ... music that totally relaxed me ... music that to this day, I still long to hear again. It was the most beautiful sound of angels singing.

Just as soon as I heard the music start, there before me stood an angel! The angel appeared to be male. His words were simple, "You will have to do what the doctors tell you to do."

I can't remember if his lips moved or if he passed the words to my mind without talking. While he spoke these words to me, I could still hear the beautiful music. My body was no longer trembling from sobbing. I was at total peace. I wasn't afraid, I wasn't angry—I wasn't anything for that moment.

I remember the music still playing for a moment longer. I had never felt so loved in my entire life. I didn't want to leave the room for fear that I would lose that "loved" feeling, which felt so wonderful and complete.

My doctors told me I would have seven months of chemotherapy and then thirty-six straight days of radiation. It was scary and difficult, but I prayed to God for courage. I prayed for strength. I prayed for the pure white light of God to heal my body. He heard my prayers and sent His angel to comfort me. I got through that time in my life and will never forget the comfort and strength I found through the help of God's love and his messenger.

ॐ Linda
New Jersey

For there stood by me this night the angel of
God, whose I am, and whom I serve.

Acts 27:23

THE CHRISTMAS ANGELS

*It was finally Christmas Eve. We had already
prepared the children as much as you can prepare
small children for something like this. It would be
their first time without anything for Christmas.*

It had been a very bad year for our family, but then it
had been bad for a lot of people that year. My husband
had not gotten a lot of work since summer, and on top of that,
he had to go to the doctor because he had a growth on his
right shoulder. It was a tumor that needed to be removed. So,
he went to a nearby Army hospital. It's a good thing we had
moved into a government housing development a few months
back; at least they wouldn't put us out on the street. I didn't
know any of the neighbors, but with four small children to
take care of, I didn't have time to make friends.

My husband was released from the hospital two weeks before
Christmas. Until this day, I don't know how the food had
lasted, but we only had a few dried beans, potatoes, cabbage,
and flour. The doctors had instructed my husband not to
go back to work, and I nearly had to fight him to keep him
from going.

It was finally Christmas Eve. We had already prepared the children, as much as you can prepare small children for something like this. It would be their first time without anything for Christmas. It must have been between five and six o'clock. We were listening to Christmas music on the radio when there was a knock at the door, and I went to answer it. Two men walked in the door and set down two huge baskets. They did not say one word; they just walked backed out. Well, my husband and I were in shock for a few seconds. My husband then said, "Hurry, catch them and thank them!" I knew that they couldn't have gotten more than just out the door, so I hurried to the door. To my surprise, they were not to be found.

We lived on a steep hill, so if they had come in by car, it would have been parked on the street below; there was no car. There were long walkways on each side; no one there, either. We asked everyone we knew if they had sent someone; they hadn't even known we were in such bad shape. When we talked about it later, we reflected on how strange those men acted and looked. So, where did they come from? Where did they go? Better yet, who were they? Well … I believe they were our Christmas angels.

It will be a Christmas we will never forget.

ঞ Kathy
Nebraska

Be not forgetful to entertain strangers; for thereby some have entertained angels unawares.

Hebrews 13:2

WALKING THROUGH THE CHAMBERS OF THE HEART

*I feel very strongly that I was allowed to help my father
because God let me walk through the chambers of his heart.*

One night, I had a dream in which I approached a one-story elementary school. I went in the door, and the room was full of children playing and laughing. I looked across the room, and there was another doorway. As I started toward it, the doorway began to distort. As I went through the doorway, it tried to close on me. I was able to get through, and it stopped closing. The second room was also full of children laughing and playing. Again, across the room, there was another doorway. As I started toward the door, this doorway also began to distort. As I went through, it again tried to close on me, but I was able to get through, and the door stopped closing. This happened again and again. Each room was full of children playing and a distorted doorway. I continued through the rooms until I had gone through the fifth door. I almost didn't make it through the fifth door, as it was bound and determined not to let me through, but I did make it, and the door froze with a small opening.

When I got into the last room, it was not a room full of children. It was a smoky tavern, dark and creepy. I noticed that my father was sitting on a barstool. I approached him and tapped him on the shoulder. He turned around and fell into my arms … I woke up in a cold sweat. I got a drink of water and went back to bed.

The next morning, my father's wife called me and told me that he had suffered a heart attack the previous night. The doctor said that they would be doing a bypass on three valves of his heart. I associated the dream with the heart attack.

At the time, I lived in Illinois, and he lived in Georgia. My father's operation would take place in Alabama. I felt it was important for me to go and stay in the hospital and pray for him during the operation. I met the surgeon and shook his hand. As he shook my hand, I felt an amazing sensation go from his hand to mine, and I felt good about him doing the surgery. When the surgery was over, the surgeon came out and told me that they had to do the bypass on five valves that were severely damaged. At that moment, the dream came back to my mind.

My father recovered and went on to live another six years. Looking back, I feel blessed knowing that I had played a small part that night in my dream by helping to keep his heart pumping so that he could have that much-needed heart surgery. I feel very strongly that I was allowed to help my father because God let me walk through the chambers of his heart.

ॐ Sylvia
Georgia

God is our refuge and strength, a very present help in trouble.
Psalm 46:1

Saved by an Angel

I raised my right hand in desperate strokes toward the shore and felt a strong hand grasp my hand.

I was hiking in the beautiful Sierra Nevada Mountains with my two daughters, Sarah and Selena. Sarah was three years old then, and Selena was just a baby, under one year of age. We were miles away from everyone.

I was carrying Selena in a baby carrier on my back as we hiked. As we went along, we came upon a reservoir that was very steep. I couldn't wade in, because the sides were too steep to stand on. The water got deep very quickly, and I knew my daughters did not know how to swim. Sarah tried to avoid the danger by walking around the reservoir's edge. As Sarah starting walking, she tripped and began rolling down the steep embankment and continued to quickly roll down about ten feet before landing in the water. She began to struggle, and each panicked move only swept her farther out into the water. I raced down to the water, trying to reach her. I finally got to her and put out my hand, reaching as far as I could toward her, but Sarah's little hand was just inches out of my reach. She quickly began moving away from the shore.

I stepped farther in this time, with water up to my waist, trying desperately to keep Selena, who was in a baby carrier on my back, out of the water. My feet then slipped into the steep reservoir, and Sarah slipped just inches out of my reach. I took another step into the water, and the steep decline caused the water to be up to my shoulders. Just as I grasped Sarah's hand, my feet slipped, and my head and my baby Selena's head also went under the water. I kicked with all my might, but I couldn't get my head above the water. I started feeling that we were all three going to drown when I desperately prayed and called out, "God, help me!" I raised my right hand in desperate strokes toward the shore and felt a strong hand grasp my hand. I was yanked along with Sarah, and with Selena still on my back, out of the water and up the ten feet to the flat land above the reservoir.

We were saved! For a moment, I just lay there, holding my daughters. I then quickly turned over to see who had miraculously saved us, only to find that no one was there. The shore was empty. We were the only ones within miles. I knew then that an angel had saved us. God heard my prayer! I continued to lie there, thanking God for sending an angel to save us.

ॐ Donald
Washington

For he shall give his angels charge over thee, to keep thee in all thy ways. They shall bear thee up in their hands, lest thou dash thy foot against a stone.

Psalm 91:11–12

Singing Angels

*Be not afraid, let your heart be light, and know that we are
with you and will be with him through this soul lesson.*

*Everything is as it should be, and our
love surrounds you both!*

From a very young age, I could see angels. Growing up
very sensitive and intuitive always made me feel a little
out of place. After years of struggling to find my true self,
I learned how to let my spiritual gifts and abilities flow. I
finally allowed myself to open up and freely offer my gifts
by performing Reiki healing and teaching others.

My son Connor was diagnosed with cancer, and it was a
pretty stressful time all across the board for my family. I
had been doing all kinds of Reiki healing work on him in
preparation for the day of his surgery, and I had been calling
in all the archangels and spirit guides to support him with
releasing his illness.

We checked into the hospital in preparation for his surgery,
and the nurses gave Connor some medicine to help him
relax just before his procedure. He was feeling pretty good

and acting a little loopy. As we waited for them to come into his room to take him into surgery, I looked up to see that the archangel Michael was standing behind his hospital bed. I could feel his warm, protective energy vibrating throughout the room. I then noticed that the archangel Gabriel was distracting Connor by singing in his ear some silly songs that Connor liked. Connor could hear them and was laughing and singing with him. It was so cute and heartwarming that I was smiling and laughing, too.

Other family members were also in the room, and because they could not hear or see the angels, I got the feeling that my behavior felt inappropriate to them … as though I should be riddled with worry because of where we were and the situation at hand. I started to pull myself together and feel a little guilty that I wasn't being more serious and praying or doing Reiki on Connor instead of enjoying the angelic presence that was with us in the room.

Just then, the archangel Raphael came up beside me and whispered these words in my ear, "To see your smile and hear your laughter is more healing to him than any service that these trained medical professionals can provide. Beam your smile and your love to your son! By doing so, you will be lifting his heart and assisting him in raising his vibration to heights where disease cannot keep its hold. He picked you to be his mother because you have the strength and love that he requires to support him on this journey of his soul. Be not afraid, let your heart be light, and know that we are with you and will be with him through this soul lesson. Everything is as it should be, and our love surrounds you both!"

These precious words given so sweetly from the archangel Raphael brought tears of joy to my eyes! I allowed myself to really smile and laugh with my son in the moments before his surgery. Connor came through his surgery just fine and is now *cancer free!*

I have held those blessed words from the archangel Raphael in my heart ever since. Because of what we've been through, I have made sure that Connor and I share as many smiles and as much gut-busting laughter as we can.

Having this gift to see and communicate with angels makes me feel as though my life is filled with divine love and magic. To be able to remember who you really are and to know that you are endowed with gifts and abilities that are just waiting to be realized is a true gift from the universe. All you have to do is be aware and feel the connection to Spirit. Lifted up by Spirit, you can be fully empowered with the divine love that we are all created from.

ॐ Karen
Michigan

I am Raphael, one of the seven angels who stand ever ready to enter the presence of the Glory of the Lord.

(Tobit 12:15) NJB (New Jerusalem Bible)

A MESSAGE OF HOPE

*I come to you with a message of hope. This message
offers you the opportunity to see your journey
here and its events through the eyes of faith.*

*Y*ears ago, I was in a very unstable and unhappy
marriage with my husband, who had slowly turned
into an alcoholic. I was doing everything that I could to try
to help him with his life, which included helping him to
start and run his own business.

He was very much against my being open with others about
my abilities to see and communicate with angels … but I
knew that I was being led to share this gift with others in
whatever capacity I could. My heart truly sang anytime
I was able to give someone information from their spirit
guides and angels. Ignoring my gifts and keeping the truth
about myself secret had been making me miserable for a long
time, and I really felt that I needed to be open about myself,
regardless of his opinion. I was very unsure about what to
do and whether my marriage would survive.

I really needed some guidance, so I called on heaven to
send me a sign or give me some guidance to help me see

my path more clearly. I went outside in my yard and sat under my favorite tree. I began with a prayer calling on Jesus, the Virgin Mary, and the angels to come near me and give me the guidance, support, healing, and inspiration that I desperately needed. I poured my heart out to my spirit guides and angels, telling them about all my thoughts, feelings, and confusion. I then let myself fall into a very peaceful meditation, allowing my worries to melt away, and I saw them gathering around me. I felt their loving presence enfolding me in divine love.

As I began to feel very happy and peaceful, surrounded by spirit, the powerful energy of the archangel Michael flowed toward me, filling up my aura. As he came into form before me, he leaned forward and laid his hands on my shoulders. He then began to speak and said, "I come to you with a message of hope. This message offers you the opportunity to see your journey here and its events through the eyes of faith. When you are able to look at your life's choices and experiences through the eyes of faith, you will see divinity in every aspect of your existence and the beauty, blessings, and synchronicity that are present even in the seemingly mundane details. Open your eyes, beloved, to your purpose in this life. Your perception of who you are in your life has been colored by the thoughts and expectations of others. Your truth and your precious heart have been held down by the wants and needs of those around you and by your fear of your own power. You are a spark from the holy flame of all creation. You hold all the answers that you seek within yourself. Learning to allow yourself to flow with the truth of who you are will open all the doors, pull back the veil, and allow divine light to shine through. I come to you now to tell you that the pain you are feeling is from hiding the light within you. The path to true happiness and peace involves letting go of your fear and trepidation. Then you will be free to shine as the holy spark that you were created to be!"

He then took me on an astral journey into my childhood, when I had first become aware that I could see and communicate with angels and spirit guides. He showed me many beautiful and truly happy memories of talking and playing with my angels as a little girl. I knew as a child that this type of communication was right for me, and it was such a special part of who I was. I understood after reliving those memories that I was always meant to be in spiritual service, to help those who were searching for a way to communicate with heaven. I was seeing my faith through Michael's eyes, and I knew what I had to do. I wasn't confused or afraid anymore … I was going to allow my light to shine.

I thanked the archangel Michael for his powerful message to me, and I began the very next day to offer my gifts openly. I have never looked back, and my life is now dedicated to serving spirit the best I can!

෨ Karen
Michigan

Be of good courage, and he shall strengthen your heart, all ye that hope in the LORD.

Psalm 31:24

MICHAEL'S PROTECTION

Your soul has chosen to stay and fulfill your divine contract.

It was early in the year, and there was still snow on the ground. There was a light dusting of snow on the roads, too—just enough to make them slick in some spots. I was traveling home from work at about 8:00 p.m., and I was singing to one of my favorite songs as I drove. I had been feeling kind of down at that time due to many issues going on all at once in my life, and I had been trying to shake the feeling of being in a rut. So, I was singing to help raise my spirits a bit, as I was going to be pulling into my driveway in less than ten minutes.

Suddenly, a small buck appeared directly in the path of my car. My first instinct was to swerve to miss him, and as I swerved, I lost control of my car. Once my tires met the snowy gravel off the road's shoulder, I felt my car being sucked down into the deep ditch. I tried slamming on my brakes and cranking my steering wheel back toward the road, but nothing was working to stop my car from careening farther into the ditch and dangerously close to several large trees. There was nothing that I could do ... so, I yelled, "Michael!"

Just then, the archangel Michael manifested as a huge violet, blue, and golden flame everywhere in my line of sight. Then everything seemed to slow down, and my car finally came to a hard stop! Both of my front airbags blew, knocking my hand off the steering wheel and scraping just past my right eye. I was dazed and breathing hard, but all the fear I had felt was gone.

As I looked around me, I saw that the front of my car was smashed against some small trees. I looked out my driver's side window to see the archangel Michael looking down at me, and he said, "Your soul has chosen to stay and fulfill your divine contract. My light and protection is with you always, and we celebrate your choice, for there is much more to come for you!"

I felt so grateful and fortunate to have the archangel Michael there with me and to hear those words from him! As his light started to dissipate, I saw that my driver's side door was three inches away from a huge oak tree. If the archangel Michael hadn't stopped my car when he did, the whole side of my car would have slammed into that tree, which probably would've killed me.

I know that my experiences here aren't always going to be pleasurable, as life on this planet can be hard. It is a wonderful journey, however, and I am very glad to be here, fulfilling my "divine contract!" I am so blessed to have such a beautiful and strong connection to the angels—especially with the archangel Michael, my divine protector, inspiration, bringer of truth, and an unlimited source of unconditional love! Thank you, Michael!

*But I will show thee that which is noted in the
scripture of truth: and [there is] none that holdeth
with me in these things, but Michael your prince.*

Daniel 10:21

Note

Learn more about Karen's spiritual and healing gifts by
contacting her or visiting her website.

&❧ Karen

Michigan

Serenity by Karen: Healing and Uplifting the Spirit

Spiritual Teacher/Reiki Master/Psychic

Serenitybykaren@yahoo.com

www.serenitybykaren.com

Go to the Light

*"Dad, is someone here?" Again, he pointed repeatedly
to the foot of his bed and nodded. I began to tremble,
for I knew what would very soon take place.*

9 had just arrived at my school that morning around 7:30 a.m., as usual, when our school secretary paged me over the intercom for an important message. *Did my husband lock himself out of the house again? Could a parent of one of my students be calling this early?* These thoughts and more flooded my mind as I raced down the hall to the office. Upon entering, out of breath, I realized something must be seriously wrong by the expression on our secretary's face. I braced myself as she firmly announced without hesitating, "Go home, Cindy. Your father is dying." As tears welled up in my eyes and overflowed, running down my flushed face, I began to realize that the fear that I had dreaded my whole life was now becoming real.

My father had been forty-two when my twin sister and I were born. Needless to say, our births had not been planned. Nine years earlier, my mother had given birth to our brother, their first born. My parents had given up on the hope of having another child. My mother, however, was still relatively young at the age of twenty-eight and hoped to become a mother once again. We were unexpected, yes, and we were certainly going to be a challenge for our parents.

There was never a time I didn't realize how proud Dad was of his twins, and we, in turn, endeavored to make him proud of us. However, I became aware at an early age that when we brought our parents to school functions, my dad was most likely the oldest parent attending. Sometimes, a few of my friends would ask, "Is that your grandpa or your dad?"

Eventually, I became very alarmed of Dad's age, and as I entered high school, I became apprehensive that we might not still have our father with us upon graduation. He would be about sixty! Now as I look back, I realize that all that worrying was needless, for I not only graduated high school with him still living; I graduated college, too, and that was seventeen years ago. I'd had many treasured years with my father upon which I hadn't counted.

With tears streaming down my face, I rushed home to gather my family and head off for my hometown to be by my father's side. In silence, my husband drove the three-hour trip while I silently prayed for God to grant me the ability to speak once more with my father before he left this earthly plane. God heard and granted my request.

Dad had been a heavy smoker throughout his life, which caused him to develop emphysema and left him with half a lung. Since my father had wrestled with two previous bouts of pneumonia that year, his strength and resistance were at the mercy of another attack. Just the night before, I had talked with him long-distance after learning of his return to the hospital once again. He assured me there was nothing to worry about and encouraged me to wait until the weekend to visit him. He didn't want me to miss school or burden anyone. That was my dad. "Sissy, I'll still be here this weekend; you can come up then," he said. We talked and laughed for nearly an hour, and I felt that I would have the weekend to be near him once more.

The stage was finally set, and the last scene was about to be played. As I rushed down the halls of the hospital to intensive care, my twin, Mindy, greeted us and informed us of his perilous condition. She explained that the doctors and staff had desperately worked, trying to bring up his blood pressure as his condition quickly deteriorated.

Quietly entering his room, I could see the lifesaving machines by his bed and a breathing tube hooked up to his mouth, which prevented him from speaking. A thin sheet covered his frail 110-pound, five-foot-nine-inch body. Dad had always been thin, but he had lost a tremendous amount of weight this year due to his reoccurring battles with pneumonia. I sat beside him, taking his hand in mine, and talked to him for a brief time, just the two of us alone in the sanitized room of machines. I felt so much now that I was the parent and he, the ill child. I knew God had generously allowed me this extra moment to talk to him about his next journey to eternity.

I gently kissed his cool brow and whispered, "Dad, do you know you're dying?" Looking deep into my eyes and trying to smile, he nodded and gazed at the foot of his bed. Trying to ease any fears he might have, I once more squeezed Dad's hand and said, "Dad, God is here and loves you, and He will lead you over to the other side. Don't be afraid." Excited, he tried to rise up; however, his strength was spent, and he fell back into his pillow, pointing to the foot of his bed and trying to mumble through the breathing tube, which prevented him from doing so.

"Dad, is someone here?" I asked. Again, he pointed repeatedly to the foot of his bed and nodded. I began to tremble, for I knew what would very soon take place. I motioned for the nurse to hurry and gather the family. As they rushed to his bedside, I looked down upon my father and realized by the glaze in his eyes that he had quietly slipped into a coma. For the next few moments, his beloved family stood by his bed and watched the machines slowly register that life was leaving my father's still body. As the last level dropped to zero, my twin cried out, "Fight, Dad, stay with us!"

At last, I patted his still hand and said, "Go to the Light, Dad; go with Him to the Light."

In three weeks, my father would have turned eighty-one years old. I know that that day, the last of my father's days on this earth, there had been someone else with us in that hospital room. It had been his angel, who took my father home to be with Jesus and to reign forever in eternity.

ઐ Cindy
Kentucky

Behold, I send an angel before thee, to keep thee in the way, and to bring thee into the place which I have prepared.

Exodus 23:20

My Angel of Love

There are those of us who believe,
many stories have been told,
that at birth you receive your very own angel to behold.
You came into this world
on a wing and a prayer,
and throughout your lifetime,
your angel was always there.
Your own guardian angel to guide you,
to watch over you,
sent from God above,
who's pure essence is love.
Then, one day, when your work on earth is done,
you will remember and regain the sight …
for you will feel God's love and see the light.
You will smile and reach for your angel's hand,
for you will be ready to go back home again.
Then you will hear the beautiful songs
and will then remember,
remember heaven's where you belong.
Angel of love,
messenger of light,
I love you and thank you for holding my hand,
and leading me back to the Promised Land.

Barbara Love